SECRET HEART OF A WORSHIPER
FROM PASTURE TO PALACE

BRIAN MING

Copyright © 2017 by Brian Ming
P.O. Box 72624
Colorado Springs, CO 80962

All rights reserved.

No part of this book may be reproduced in any form or by any electronic or mechanical means, including information storage and retrieval systems, without written permission from the author, except for the use of brief quotations in a book review.

Unless otherwise indicated, all Scripture quotations are taken from the Holy Bible, New Living Translation, copyright © 1996, 2004, 2007, 2013, 2015 by Tyndale House Foundation. Used by permission of Tyndale House Publishers, Inc., Carol Stream, Illinois 60188. All rights reserved.

Scripture quotations marked (HCSB®) are taken from the Holman Christian Standard Bible®, Copyright © 1999, 2000, 2002, 2003, 2009 by Holman Bible Publishers. Used by permission. HCSB® is a federally registered trademark of Holman Bible Publishers.

Scripture quotations marked (KJV) are taken from the Holy Bible, King James Version (Public Domain).

Scripture quotations marked (NASB) are taken from the New American Standard Bible®, Copyright © 1960, 1962, 1963, 1968, 1971, 1972, 1973, 1975, 1977, 1995 by The Lockman Foundation. Used by permission.

Scripture quotations marked (NIV) are taken from the Holy Bible, New International Version®, NIV®. Copyright © 1973, 1978, 1984, 2011 by Biblica, Inc.™ Used by permission of Zondervan. All rights reserved worldwide. www.zondervan.com The "NIV" and "New International Version" are trademarks registered in the United States Patent and Trademark Office by Biblica, Inc.™

Scripture quotations marked (NKJV) are taken from the New King James Version®. Copyright © 1982 by Thomas Nelson. Used by permission. All rights reserved.

Scripture quotations marked (TLB) are taken from The Living Bible copyright © 1971. Used by permission of Tyndale House Publishers, Inc., Carol Stream, Illinois 60188. All rights reserved.

Scripture quotations marked (MSG) are taken from The Message. Copyright © by Eugene H. Peterson 1993, 1994, 1995, 1996, 2000, 2001, 2002. Used by permission of NavPress. All rights reserved. Represented by Tyndale House Publishers, Inc.

Edited by Edie Mourey (www.furrowpress.com).

ISBN-13: 978-1-5423-5558-2

Created with Vellum

When I think about a worshiper, one person comes to mind more than any other: my wife. As a child she was continually encouraged by her family, "Sing to Jesus." Like David in the pasture, long before the limelight of a stage or microphone, she learned how to worship God with passion and purity of heart. Her lifestyle of worship has taught me more about the secret heart of a worshiper than any other. I love you, babe!

CONTENTS

Introduction	1
Week 1 *Shepherd Boy*	3
Week 2 *Shepherd Warrior*	27
Week 3 *Zero to Hero*	55
Week 4 *Friend or Foe?*	85
Week 5 *Outlaw on the Run*	115
Week 6 *Cave Experiences*	137
Week 7 *New Wives*	163
Week 8 *Hiding among Enemies*	189
Week 9 *From Pasture to Palace*	211
About the Author	237
Also by Brian Ming	239

INTRODUCTION

Several years ago, I felt compelled to start keeping a journal. For the first several months, I wasn't very good at it. I didn't write anything too deep. Instead, I kept a running narrative of my daily activities. Then, life started happening. Things became a little more interesting than the day-to-day monotony I had been experiencing. Questions related to what I was going through suddenly drove my journal entries—questions like: "How did I end up here?" or, "What in the world is going on?" Sometimes, I was even so bold as to ask, "Where are You, God?" or, "How could You let this happen?"

Over time, what started as a daily journal has become my lifeblood—my deepest reflections, prayers, and worship. Often, I find myself getting lost in journaling and worshiping God for hours.

I've always been fascinated with the life of David. From an early age, I heard about the shepherd boy who defeated a Philistine giant with a slingshot. Over my years in ministry as a worship leader, I learned David's rise to power under King Saul was turbulent, but it wasn't until teaching a class on Psalms that I discovered how much of David's journey correlated to his worship life.

One day, while reading through the Psalms, I couldn't help but notice how similar they were to my journal entries. Without realizing it, like David, in pure real-time emotion, I had penned my heart—often writing songs in the process.

I'm not alone. Many lovers of the Psalms relate to David's real-time transparency throughout. His worship in the midst of trials and tragedy also gives us a glimpse into the heart of Israel's giant slayer and future king.

David is celebrated for being a man after God's own heart. As I studied for the class, I couldn't help but wonder: *What does that mean?* I believe the Psalms (what I consider David's journal) hold the answers.

In the pages ahead, you will hear about the life of Israel's shepherd king in, perhaps, a way you've never heard before. This journal expresses what David might have felt and internalized on his journey from lowly shepherd to the sung about king of Israel. As David learned, anyone chosen for a monumental task will encounter significant difficulties, rejection, and opposition. In David's response we learn the *Secret Heart of a Worshiper*.

WEEK 1
SHEPHERD BOY

DAY 1: MONDAY
1 SAMUEL 16:6–12

David was just an average kid, the youngest of eight brothers. He was full of life and energy and, as with all kids, had his mischievous moments. He did all the usual stuff—horseplay with his friends and brothers, and hunting rodents with his slingshot—and he played his harp.

At a very young age, David learned the art of not only fending for himself but also defending himself. Being the baby of the family wasn't easy, as his older siblings often picked on and pestered him. They did, however, teach him the family trade. He easily took to it and quickly became very good at it.

By the time he was a young teenager, David's dad had turned him loose to handle jobs on his own. Even more than his older brothers, David had a knack for knowing what to do in complicated and trying situations. He was quick-witted, handsome, and knowledgeable far beyond his years.

Being talented and responsible came with a price. On occasion, David's dad gave him dangerous tasks spanning over far distances. Unfortunately, David's being gone alone so much resulted in his being out of sight, out of mind, and thus overlooked by his dad and brothers.

David began taking his harp along on the most difficult jobs and found solace in his music. He played every time he had the chance and, before long, became a prolific musician and singer, even composing songs. The music and songs were his outlet and ultimately became his strength.

Out in the open air, under the stars, he sang and played not just to fill time but also to worship his God. And for that reason, the hardships he faced were a blessing in disguise.

One day, things dramatically changed for the hardworking teen. He was called in from his duties by his older brother, "Hey, David, come with me—*quickly*! Someone is here to see you."

David dropped what he was doing, and to his surprise, a holy man was visiting their family. This was no ordinary man of God but the chief prophet of the nation. His name was Samuel. In a hurry, having run all the way there, David was winded. The well-known prophet didn't wait for him to catch his breath. As soon as Samuel saw him, Samuel raised a flask of oil and poured it over his head. The prophet's action foretold David would become king.

How exhilarating and, at the same time, how dreadful for the young lad. Singled out in the presence of his older brothers and his father, God had selected David, not for a small task, but to be king over the entire nation! The prophet's anointing him should have been an honor enjoyed by the entire family, but it was difficult for his seven brothers because the prophet had chosen David and not any of them.

From that very day, each of his older siblings kept a jealous eye upon David. The ridiculing never stopped. They ranked on him by calling him, "Your Excellency," or, "Your Majesty." Although he hated the awful teasing, their snide comments helped him develop a tenacious spirit. David was forced to be strong and resilient. Of course, that wasn't new—not for the runt of the family, not for the overlooked one, and especially not for the next king of Israel.

Although David fell into many fits of depression, he learned how to lift himself up through song. He learned how to rise above the opposition he faced. And most of all, he learned how to depend on his God—relying on a supernatural strength that came from one place: worship.

Sitting in the meadow, once again on the job, he used the time to practice his slingshot, play his harp, and sing to the Lord his God. Little did David know the next phase of his journey—leading to more brokenness—was about to begin.

DAY 2: TUESDAY
1 SAMUEL 17:28

"What do you think you're doing, David?" Eliab scolded. "Just because you think you're better than us doesn't mean you can skip out on your shepherding duties."

David didn't respond, not wanting to betray his thoughts.

Shimea laughed and tossed him a shepherd's staff. "Your scepter, My Liege."

The teasing and David's being left to tend the sheep on his own were getting old. *Where are those brothers of mine off to anyway?* David had a sneaking suspicion where his older brothers were going. They'd been asking—no—begging their father for permission to enlist in the King's Army. David had overheard several people from town talking about it. He was young but not too young to fight. He could certainly hold his own. He knew it.

His father had heard the prophet, so David didn't understand why his dad hadn't suggested he join the army. *If anyone should go,* he thought, *it should be me. I should go and sign up.*

Joining the King's Army seemed logical. It seemed like the right thing to do, especially if Samuel were right about David's being next in line. *But didn't the king have a son? Wasn't Jonathan next in line?* Every question he had only led to more questions.

A bit flustered, David grabbed his staff and slingshot, strapped his harp on his back, and headed out. *Another shepherd duty, ugh!* It seemed like that's all he was good for lately. *How is this relevant?* he wondered. *What good am I doing here with the sheep?*

After grazing and watering the flock, he plopped down under a cypress tree. Even in the shade, David was profusely sweating in the desert climate. He was tired and frustrated. But that hadn't stopped him before, and it wouldn't now. He took his harp, and he began playing a familiar tune, a song he'd heard and learned that Moses had supposedly written. He soon sang the words to the song, "Lord, through all the generations You have been our home! Before the mountains were born, before You gave birth to the earth and the world, from beginning to end, You are God" (Ps 90:1–2).

David stopped and looked around. He saw mountains off in the distance. *Wow,* he marveled, *before the mountains were born or the earth was formed—You were there, Lord. You were present. You created them just the way they are. And You created me just the way I am.*

David then scolded himself for having been frustrated earlier. It led him to pray aloud, "I'm sorry, Lord, for fretting over this mundane job. I'm grateful that You chose me for a future task. Help me to be faithful to my father's wishes even when I don't understand what You're doing in my life."

David began playing and singing again. He was starting to feel better when a noise in the distance startled him. He stood up and looked around. There was something out there. Something was rustling off far away in the bushes. The sheep stirred. David gulped, dropped his harp, and picked up his staff and slingshot.

A lion—it was a lion! Any hireling would have run away, but David was no hireling. Voice trembling, he prayed, "Rescue me from the mouth of the lions" (Ps 22:21 NIV).

DAY 3: WEDNESDAY
1 SAMUEL 11:6–7; 16:14–20; 17:34–37

From the moment David slew the lion, he knew something had definitely changed. Whatever Samuel had poured over him must have been magic oil. He had heard the stories of Sampson, how the Spirit of God came upon him and empowered him to kill lions, carry city gates, and wreak havoc on thousands of Philistines.

Was this what it was like? He mused, *Was this the power of the Spirit of God Almighty?*

Deep down, he knew it was. Yes, something had drastically changed, yet he couldn't quite explain it.

David remembered a more recent event when the Spirit had overshadowed King Saul, resulting in the king's prophesying. The people had joked, "Is Saul among the prophets?" Only a month later, the king had heard about the Ammonites besieging the Israelite city of Jabesh-Gilead, and he had been furious. The Spirit of God had come upon King Saul, and he had taken a team of oxen and cut them in pieces. He had sent the pieces throughout the territory of Israel by the hand of messengers who had said, "This is what will be done to the oxen of anyone who does not follow Saul and Samuel" (1 Sam 11:6–7 NIV).

The people had known this was serious. The fear of the Lord had come over them, and they had assembled as one. It had happened! Samuel's appointment of Saul was confirmed, and from that moment Saul had come into his divine calling as king.

Standing over the carcass of the lion he had killed, something clicked in David's mind. In an instant, he realized, *God has anointed me just as He anointed Saul.*

In awe, David dusted himself off and returned to gather the scattering sheep. He wiped the wet blood from the scratches on his arms. Although the beast was dead, David had not gone unscathed by the encounter. *What have I got myself into here?* David wondered. *Was this preparation? Training?*

From that point on, shepherding took on a whole new meaning to him. When David returned from the flocks that day, his brothers noticed the difference right away. Their snooty remarks didn't seem to faze him anymore. Yes, David was changing, not only in his own eyes but in the eyes of all those around him. His wisdom increased, and, like a magnet, his leadership drew others to him. He fought battles—although small and seemingly insignificant—but always won. Over time, he became known for his bravery. Most of all, people realized that God was with him.

David continued shepherding and faithfully serving his father. Meanwhile, an evil spirit from God began to torment King Saul. And unbeknown to David, a servant from the region of Bethlehem who had enlisted in Saul's army gave an important recommendation to the king.

It was a day like any other when David received the word, "The king needs your services." And as Pharaoh had summoned Joseph, King Saul summoned David, not by his own doing but by the Lord's.

David's time had come—or had it?

DAY 4: THURSDAY
1 SAMUEL 16:23; 17:15

David's heart raced as he approached the king's tent for the first time. The servant who had called on him also prepped him on their way there. Certain protocols were in place. David was told: "Only speak when spoken to," and, "When the king's anger begins to flare up, that's your cue."

David didn't know what to expect. Perhaps, the king would be cordial, or maybe he wouldn't be. From what David had been told, the king probably wouldn't be. After all, he had more important things to do than ensure all the questions of a minstrel like David were answered. Knowing that, however, didn't keep David's mind from questioning, *Will I be on center stage or off in a corner somewhere, out of sight and out of the way?* David was certainly used to being overlooked, playing an insignificant role that nobody seemed to notice.

As he suspected, David was asked to set up in the corner. He never spoke directly to the king. And yet, when David played, the evil spirit left the king's presence. Everyone noticed that Saul was happier when the young shepherd boy was playing. The king seemed somewhat pacified as he didn't lose his temper as often and slept a lot better.

David worshiped and watched. He watched and worshiped. Without even realizing it (or maybe he did), he had a bird's eye view of how the kingdom worked, how battle strategies were drawn up, and how Saul interacted with those around him. David gained a perspective on the inner workings of the kingdom even generals in the army didn't have. All the while, nobody noticed, and nobody cared.

During his time in King Saul's service, David wrote:

> Now I know that the Lord rescues His anointed king. He will answer him from His holy heaven and rescue him by His great power. Some nations boast of their chariots and horses, but we boast in the name of the Lord our God. Those nations will fall down and collapse, but we will rise up and stand firm. Give victory to our king, O Lord! (Ps 20:6-9).

David felt important. He thought: *I'm on my way. It's all lining up, just like Samuel said it would. I am here—in the king's tent with King Saul.* He had left his brothers and the shepherd fields far behind.

Although David resisted the urge, sometimes he relished: *If my brothers could see me now.* He wanted to rub their noses in his promotion. *See, I told you so.*

Unfortunately, as quick as his service began, it was over. Jesse sent word that he needed David back in Bethlehem. Not knowing why his father needed him, he was given permission to return to Bethlehem, back to home, back to shepherding, and back to his brothers.

DAY 5: FRIDAY
1 SAMUEL 17:13–14, 34–37

Upon David's return, Eliab and his brothers bowed to pay homage. "The king has returned," they joked. David rolled his eyes and headed out to do his daily tasks. He had been in the king's service for some time, but that was then. He was home now, and that meant it was back to his usual run-of-the-mill routine. Chores were completed, food was prepared and eaten, and—last but not least—more shepherding was needed.

How exciting it had been to be among the regiment of the king. It was fast-paced. They were making a difference—fighting wars that mattered—and saving lives. In David's absence, his brothers had picked up the slack. And David knew what that meant: He was expected to do extra work to make up for the time he had been away.

Sure enough, David spent a week or more on the open plain watching his father's flock. He was alone once again, or was he?

No matter where David found himself, God was there. He looked past the flock to the open plains, clutched his harp and began to play. He couldn't get away from shepherding. It was what he had done since a youth, and with that thought and the plucking of a few strings came this song:

> The Lord is my shepherd, I shall not want. He makes me to lie down in green pastures, He leads me beside still waters. He leads me in paths of righteousness for His name's sake. Yea, though I walk through the valley of the shadow of death Your rod and Your staff comfort me (Ps 23:1–3 NKJV).

David had been through many dangerous situations in the pasture. He thought about the lion he had faced and how God had given him victory. He thought about the wolves he had fended off. As if on cue, all at once, another predator came upon him. This time, it was a bear.

David jumped up and ran toward the scary beast and, with sling in hand, hurled a rock at it. Unfortunately, the rock did little besides make the bear angrier and more aggressive.

The bear turned and faced him. David froze, and his eyes met those of his adversary. Sheep bleated away, but David stood his ground. One thing he knew: *God, if You don't help me now, I'm a goner.* Reaching down to the ground, slowly and cautiously, he picked up another stone. Unlike the other rock he had hurled, this one was smooth.

The bear growled, grunted, and beat at the ground with its huge paws. Dust rose in a cloud around the animal. In a split second, and to David's horror, the beast began charging. With a mighty thrust, David swung his sling and let the rock fly. It crashed into the animal's large head with a loud *smack!*

Adrenaline rushed through David's body as he braced for the attack and prepared to defend himself. The bear, however, ran only a few more steps before dropping to the ground—flat. Running over to the animal, David struck the beast in the head several times with his staff. It didn't move, just convulsed and twitched. Making sure it was dead, David cut its throat. Blood poured onto the ground.

It was over.

"Welcome back," David muttered under his breath. It was odd how he had felt safer during war in the king's service than here in the wilderness. Twice now, God had helped him triumph over the beasts of the field. And he knew that no matter where he found himself, he was in constant need of God's provision and of God's strength and courage.

God, You are my shepherd. You are my protector in the valley of the shadow of death. David realized it was more than a song. In song, he had been declaring God's promises. And in truth, he was under God's direction as *his* shepherd.

After tending to the sheep for several more days, David finally headed home. As he arrived back to his father's house, he sensed something new in the air. It was quieter than usual, chillingly quiet. Was his mother crying?

"What's going on?" David asked one of the servant boys.

"Haven't you heard?" the boy asked. "Your older brothers have enlisted in the army. They've gone off to fight against the Philistine threat with King Saul."

David had once again been overlooked. He felt farther away from the kingdom than ever before. David's heart sank with a tired sigh, knowing what that meant. It wasn't his father—but his Heavenly Shepherd—who once again left him out.

DAY 6: SATURDAY
REFLECTIONS FROM THE WEEK

Malachi described God as a *refiner's fire*. It's a common phrase used in sermons, teachings, songs, and even prayers. I've asked the Lord to burn away the dross in my life, to come as a refiner's fire. At the time, I had no idea what I was asking for. And I never considered how difficult the process would be. To be refined, gold must be placed in a furnace of fire until the fire burns away all the imperfections. Only then is it considered *pure* gold.

Our earliest encounter with David comes from 1 Samuel 15, where the prophet Samuel traveled to the town of Bethlehem to anoint Saul's replacement as the next king of Israel. By divine insight, Samuel knew he would anoint someone from the house of Jesse. The prophet was aware of the customs of the day, which favored the firstborn, and he was automatically drawn to Jesse's oldest son, Eliab. He was at least seven years older than David and already of age for consideration.

God, however, did something that surprised the prophet. During the feast, God told Samuel, "Do not look at his appearance or at the height of his stature ... for God sees not as man sees, for man looks at the outward appearance, but the Lord looks at the heart" (1 Sam 16:7 NASB).

Eliab was rejected, along with Abinadab, Shimea, and the rest of their brothers. Samuel stood back perplexed. Had he missed God? After careful recollection of God's instructions, he was sure the future king would be from this family line, so he asked Jesse, "Is there another son?"

"Yes, there is—the youngest," Jesse replied. "He's out with the sheep."

Our first introduction to David from his father's perspective is this: In Jesse's mind, the boy wasn't worthy of attending the important event.

I don't see this as coincidence. God knew the boy wouldn't be invited. He made a point to exclude him, and thus, David's refining process, development, and preparation had officially begun.

After being called in from the pasture, Samuel anointed David in the presence of his brothers. I've often wondered why God did it this way? Why not just send Samuel alone out to the shepherd field? Why not allow Samuel to anoint David without his family present? It's simple. David was singled out and only chosen after his brothers were *not* chosen. Then, in the presence of his brothers, Samuel anointed David.

As with Joseph centuries earlier, we know that being singled out (chosen and favored) by God leads to much rejection. Jesse and his brothers didn't forge a crown and place a sword in David's hand while shouting, "Long live the king!" In fact, not a single person rallied behind him. Instead, after being anointed, David continued in the service of his father's household as a shepherd.

David was certainly a *boy* with a good pliable heart for God. But being singled out by the prophet didn't automatically make him a *man* after God's own heart. In extensively studying the life of David,

I can't think of a better example of how God took someone with potential (and even a heart for God) and, through the fire of adversity, refined him into someone great.

Maybe you're in a hard place. Perhaps, you're doing mundane, seemingly meaningless, work. And yet, you feel—and deep down know—God has destined you for greatness. Don't be surprised by difficult circumstances. Don't be surprised when you are mistreated and encounter jealousy. Oh, and don't be surprised if your greatest opposition comes from those closest to you, such as family members, close friends, or trusted ministry leaders. Know that it's a part of the refining process. God uses the fire of rejection to remove the impurities in you. You will not be as pure as gold until you go through the furnace of fire. David did. Joseph did. Peter and the disciples did. Paul the apostle did. And so will you.

David's refining wasn't comfortable or pleasant. And yet, we can use his journey to help us find strength in the presence of God. Read through the Psalms and realize that, many times, David was crying out to God from a place of anguish.

DAY 7: SUNDAY
A CLOSER LOOK AT PSALM 22

Psalm 22 is best known as David's *Messianic Psalm*. Jesus quoted the opening line while on the cross: "My God, my God, why have You forsaken me?" (Matt 27:46 NIV). Other prophetic references in Psalm 22 include:

My life is poured out like water, and all my bones are out of joint (v 14).

My enemies surround me like a pack of dogs; an evil gang closes in on me. They have pierced my hands and feet (v 16).

They divide my garments among themselves and throw dice for my clothing (v 18).

How astounding and accurate was David's account of the way the future Messiah would be treated. How could David have known? The truth is, he didn't. He didn't have any idea what he was singing about but was only responding to his own pain. I've often said, "Those with the most pain make the best worshipers."

Jesus' statement about a sinful woman confirms this truth: "Her many sins have been forgiven; that's why she loved much. But the one who is forgiven little, loves little" (Luke 7:47 HCSB).

One thing is certain about Psalm 22. In dramatic fashion, David took time to reflect on his many hardships. Such hardships were endured from his early years as he wrote:

> But I am a worm and not a man, scorned by mankind and despised by the people. All who see me mock me (v 6 NIV).
>
> Yet You are He who took me from the womb; You made me trust You at my mother's breasts (v 9 NIV).
>
> I was cast upon You from birth; from my mother's womb You have been my God. Do not be far from me, for trouble is near; And there is no one to help (vv 10–11 NIV).

From humble beginnings to eventually becoming king over God's people, Israel, David learned how to find strength in his God, not in man, during the most difficult times of his journey.

At the close of Week 1, read these excerpts from Psalm 22, meditate on them, and make them your prayer. You may well find strength as David did.

> You are holy, enthroned on the praises of Israel. In You our fathers trusted; they trusted, and You delivered them. To You they cried and were rescued; in You they trusted and were not put to shame (vv 3–5).

Save me from the mouth of the lion! You have rescued me from the horns of the wild oxen! I will tell of Your name to my brothers; in the midst of the congregation I will praise You: You who fear the Lord, praise Him! All you . . . , glorify Him, and stand in awe of Him. . . . For He has not despised or abhorred the affliction of the afflicted, and He has not hidden His face from him, but has heard, when he cried to Him. From You comes my praise in the great congregation; my vows I will perform before those who fear Him. The afflicted shall eat and be satisfied; those who seek Him shall praise the Lord! (vv 21–26).

WEEK 2
SHEPHERD WARRIOR

DAY 8: MONDAY
1 SAMUEL 17:15, 17–24

Time seemed to stand still, not just for David but for his entire family. News from the war was hard to get. Although proud of his eldest sons, Jesse couldn't help but worry. So did David, but for other reasons.

Of course, he was concerned for his brothers, but he questioned himself, *What am I doing here?* His heart was torn. He wanted to be where the action was. His destiny was with the kingdom. He had an in-road to the king, and yet there he sat, holding a staff instead of a sword.

David threw his slingshot down on a rock and kicked the dirt. Some sheep reacted, scurrying away. He took notice of how thick and heavy their coats were. Sheering season was not far off. *Ugh!*

After grazing the flock, he led them down to the spring for water. Later at dusk, while still with the sheep, David looked up and saw a servant coming. *I wonder what he wants?*

David ran to him, "Any word from the war?" he asked. "Is everything okay?"

"No news," the servant replied. "I'm here to relieve you. Your father is worried and has asked you to come home immediately."

David wasn't surprised. He had seen stress take its toll on his father, especially as of late. After arriving home, he was given the following instructions from his dad,

> Take this ephah of roasted grain and these ten loaves of bread for your brothers and hurry to their camp. Take along these ten cheeses to the commander of their unit. See how your brothers are and bring back some assurance from them. They are with Saul and all the men of Israel in the Valley of Elah (1 Sam 17:17—19).

The next morning, David gathered all the items and started out towards Israel's camp. Soon, he stopped. In his haste to leave, he had forgotten his slingshot. Traveling across the countryside was dangerous. Thieves and bandits could appear at any time, especially if carrying goods. He had his harp to be of any service to the king while he was there, but he didn't have his sling.

I guess I can do without it. David tried to continue on, but something kept gnawing at his gut—*Go get it. You're going to need it.*

David couldn't figure it out. What would he possibly need his slingshot for? He was heading to war, not to a competition. If anything, he might bring a sword along. He was no expert swordsman, but he could manage, hold his own if need be. Another quarter mile up the road, David finally gave into the nagging feeling and returned home to retrieve his slingshot.

Finally, he was off for good. Excitement and adrenaline rushed through his veins. At last, he would be close to where the action was. At last, he was back where he was supposed to be—in the kingdom.

The closer he came to where the army was camped, the more chatter he heard. Everyone on the road was talking about it, "The army has been camped across the lines of the Philistine army for forty days now." He was surprised. *Forty days and not a single battle. That's odd.*

Another traveler told him, "The Philistine champion—Goliath—has challenged King Saul to a one-on-one duel. But the king hasn't accepted." Champion warfare wasn't uncommon. Instead of a massive fight, the outcome of the battle was decided by a one-on-one duel. Israel's champion against Philistine's champion. Winner takes all.

David had seen the king in close quarters. He was huge. And everybody said he was a great fighter. *I wonder why Saul has not offered to fight?*

As David approached the Israeli camp, a knot began to form in the pit of his stomach. For some odd reason, he felt God's presence in a powerful way, almost as if God was guiding him there. Although his head was telling him he was just a delivery boy, something else was letting him know he was marching into battle. It was strange.

David shook it off and began asking around for his brothers. In a camp of multiplied thousands, he figured it could take him awhile to find them. David searched for an hour to no avail. Finally, someone told him his brothers were down by the frontlines. Heading in their direction, he couldn't help but notice the great throng camped across the valley. It was the Philistines, and their vast presence was sobering. He had never seen such a large encampment. The tension was high. He felt it in the air.

What's wrong with everyone? David wondered. The Israelites looked discouraged. He couldn't figure out why everyone seemed afraid. These men were the army of God, were they not? God Almighty was on their side. How could they lose against a pagan force—even a vast host like that before them?

After locating his brothers, David made a beeline for them. On his way, something—someone else—caught his attention. The largest man David had ever seen, with armor shining brightly in the sun, was standing on the open battlefield. He began shouting and waving his massive spear in the air. David figured the giant must be the Philistine warrior he had heard about. *This must be Goliath. What is everybody afraid of?*

DAY 9: TUESDAY
1 SAMUEL 17:26–31

A ppearance was terrifying, but not nearly as ghastly as what he was saying. That's what made David's blood boil.

In a deep bellowing tone, Goliath shouted, "Give me a man who will fight me! Are you not Saul's men?" He spat on the ground and beat his shield on his chest. "If your God is so powerful, why not send a man to come fight me? Maybe Saul is scared. Yeah, he's scared. That's what I think!"

Pangs of heat worked their way up the nape of David's neck. Goliath wasn't just taunting the Israeli army or King Saul; he was defying God Almighty. Furious, David turned and asked someone around him, "What is everybody afraid of?"

"Of *him*," a man said, trembling. "Don't you see him? He's a giant!"

David reached his brothers, offering them the food he had brought. "How goes the war?" he asked. "Who is this giant that keeps defying the living God? And why has no one gone out to fight him?"

David's brothers rolled their eyes at him. "You wouldn't understand," Eliab retorted.

Then, David did something out of character. He left his three brothers he hadn't seen in months, turned to some men standing beside them, and asked, "What will be done for the man who defeats Goliath?"

The men replied, "The king will give great wealth to the man who kills him. He will also give him his daughter in marriage and will exempt his family from paying taxes."

"Oh, is that so?" David replied, stroking his chin. He felt conflicted. He knew the prophet had forecasted his fate. What better way to jumpstart his destiny than by becoming a war hero *and*, even more importantly, the king's son-in-law? At that moment, David was fully aware of the opportunity before him.

Eliab overheard him asking questions and said, "Why have you come down here? And with whom did you leave those few sheep in the wilderness? I know how conceited you are and how wicked your heart is; you came down only to watch the battle" (1 Sam 17:28).

Figures. Eliab's statement epitomized how he and his brothers felt about David. David's attempts to rise above hadn't gone unnoticed. Without a second thought, he blurted, "Can't I even speak?" Immediately, he turned away to ask someone else, "What did you say the prize was for killing the giant?"

Eliab's response infuriated David, pushing him over the edge. *I'll show them once and for all.* He had no time to bother with his jealous brothers. An opportunity was right here, right now. *This is it. This is what I've been waiting for—preparing for.*

To David's amazement, his willingness to fight Goliath found its way back to the king. And it wasn't long until David stood before Saul to give an account for his claims.

DAY 10: WEDNESDAY
1 SAMUEL 17:32–37

On his way to Saul's tent, David wondered, *What am I going to tell the king?* David knew this was a point of no return—a crossroad in his journey. *How can I convince the king to let me fight the giant?*

David held tight to his slingshot, nervously wringing his fingers over the leather. It was rough and worn from use. He was an expert marksman, but what good would a slingshot do against the likes of a warrior such as Goliath? And yet, the thought that steeled David's mind was one of disdain—of righteous anger. *How could the warriors of Israel be so cowardly concerning this uncircumcised Philistine?* That was the real issue here. David seemed to hold a different perspective than everyone—including Saul. An internal wrestling match was twisting his bowels as he contemplated what he was about to do.

As he arrived at the king's tent and his moment was soon to be upon him, he figured he would do one of two things: He would either grab hold of his divine destiny or shy away from it as everyone else had. David looked around and caught a glimpse of the cowering faces about him. It made him feel ashamed. Suddenly, the prize King

Saul was offering didn't matter. David understood there was something more important at stake. Something rose up in his heart and seemed to spark a fire inside him: *If they're not willing to fight the pagan giant, I will.*

That led David to his original quandary of how he was going to convince the king to let him fight Goliath. A moment before entering the king's tent, David ran his hand over a scar on his forearm he had received while fighting the lion. He remembered how God had supernaturally empowered him to bring down the large cat. And suddenly, David knew what he was to say.

Several military commanders stopped what they were doing. Saul's back was to David. He turned and looked curiously at the young shepherd. "David?" the king asked, walking over to him.

"Yes, Sire," David replied.

The king looked tired, more tired than David had ever seen him. Dark circles hung below his bloodshot eyes. Saul took a long look at the young shepherd. David read his facial expressions and knew what he was thinking.

"I will go and fight Goliath," David said. "I will fight him and defeat him!"

Scoffing laughter around the room made the embarrassed king look at the ground. How he had hoped the rumor was true—that a man was willing to take on the giant—but before him stood only an overzealous boy, probably looking to make a name for himself.

"That's a lofty claim, given that Goliath has been a man of war since before you were even born," the king chided. "What makes you think you have what it takes to defeat this giant twice your age—and twice your height?" the king added with a hint of sarcasm. His commanders laughed out loud, seemingly amused by the situation.

David knew his opportunity had arrived. Seizing his destiny was now or never. "King Saul, I know I'm just a boy in your sight—and in the sight of your men. But please hear me out before you discount what I have to say."

Saul looked around and motioned for his commanders to hush before he sat down. "What can it hurt," the king said. "Continue."

David cleared his throat and gathered himself and then flashed a confident look to those standing around. "How many of you have killed a lion with nothing more than a staff and a sling? Anyone?" The air was sucked out of the room as David stared into the now bewildered eyes of his betters, their faces flush and pale. "How about a bear?"

David turned and squarely looked the king in the eyes, "Your servant has been keeping his father's sheep. When a lion or a bear came and carried off a sheep from the flock, I went after it, struck it, and rescued the sheep from its mouth. When it turned on me, I seized it by its hair, struck it, and killed it. Your servant has killed both the lion and the bear."

Saul's jaw fell open. He shifted uncomfortably and looked around the room at his men. His eyes met Abner's. David knew Abner was Saul's chief military commander. David turned to him and said, "Here, I have the scars on my arms to prove it. Look at my arms."

Abner inspected David's arm and nodded to Saul.

David's voice grew fiery with passion, "This uncircumcised Philistine will be like one of them because he has defied the armies of the living God! The Lord who rescued me from the paw of the lion and the paw of the bear will rescue me from the hand of this Philistine."

All eyes turned to the king who was stewing in his thoughts. Abner spoke up, "What do you say, my King? Do we really want to place our hope in the hands of this untrained shepherd boy?"

Saul stood and stared into David's eyes. The boy stared back—jaw clenched—as if ready to pounce upon the giant even now. To everyone's surprise, including David's, Saul looked at his military leader and announced, "Yes, I will let you fight the Philistine champion." The words seemed to sting his throat as they came out. Saul looked at David and said, "Yes, go and fight Goliath, and God be with you."

Utter shock and disbelief filled the room. Abner put his hand on Saul's shoulder, "My King, are you—"

Saul shrugged it off. "I've made my decision, General!"

"Go and may God give you the victory—for all our sakes," Saul said to David before dismissing him.

David turned to exit the tent. Before he could leave, Saul yelled to him, "David, wait! Before you go, I have something for you."

King Saul walked over to a large wooden chest in the corner. As he opened it, the silence was interrupted by a loud *creak*. "Here," he told David. "Take my armor and my sword. You're going to need them."

DAY 11: THURSDAY
1 SAMUEL 17:38–40

Saul dressed David in his own tunic. He put his coat of armor on David and a bronze helmet on his head. David fastened on the king's sword over the tunic and tried walking around. He felt clumsy and off balance.

"Now, you're ready to fight," Saul said.

What do I do? David pondered. Deep down, he knew the armor and sword were not for him. He had already been given permission to fight on the king's behalf. But wearing the king's protective gear and brandishing the king's sword would not do.

David had come this far, and, although he didn't want to offend the king, he had to be honest. And, then, the thought hit him: *Am I fighting on behalf of King Saul, or am I fighting on behalf of the Lord of Hosts?*

He didn't have to ask for the king's permission. He could have snuck onto the battlefield and fought the giant, but that wouldn't have been right. Saul was king, and David was not. Somehow, David knew he had to get the king's blessing. And he now had it.

With the blessing, however, David knew he must step onto the battlefield as he was, not as Saul had beckoned him to be. David sensed there was a boundary being forged. Besides, shouldn't the king have been fighting in his place, yet for some reason he was unwilling?

David removed the bronze helmet. He was about to abandon the sword when he thought: *How will I defeat the champion without a sword?* David didn't know. He handed the sword to his master and said, "I'm sorry, King, but I can't go in these. They don't feel right. This is not how I will defeat the giant. I must go without them."

Saul looked appalled. "What? No, here, take them. You'll need them."

David was determined. He said firmly, "I simply cannot. But I will go and fight. And I will win!"

Saul was hesitant but finally relented. The unsure look in his eyes made his men nervous—especially Abner. Even with reservation, the king's word prevailed. And with his blessing, Saul released David to fight the Philistine champion.

Slowly and cautiously, David made his way to the battlefield. His eyes met Abinadab's, then Shimea's, and lastly Eliab's. Their eyes were wide and white, filled with shock and disbelief. Were they rooting for him? Of course, they were. The heathen giant was a threat to all of God's people. And they would root for—hope for—victory over all of Israel's adversaries, even if it came at the hand of their stubborn young brother.

David paused at the creek, bent down, and selected five smooth stones. Then he prayed: "Praise the Lord, who is my Rock. He trains my hands for war. . . . He is my loving ally and my fortress, my tower of safety, my rescuer. He is my shield, and I take refuge in Him" (Ps 144:1–2).

David looked out and saw the Philistine champion and his armor bearer and prayed to God Almighty: "Bend down the heavens, Lord, and come. . . . Let loose Your lightning bolts, Your arrows, Lord, upon Your enemies, and scatter them. Reach down from heaven and rescue me; deliver me from deep waters, from the power of my enemies" (Ps 144:5–7 MSG).

David stood, trusting—knowing—God was with him.

DAY 12: FRIDAY
1 SAMUEL 17:41–53

The sun was hot, but David did not notice. He focused on one thing—one man. As he approached Goliath, getting closer and closer, he saw how mammoth the Philistine was. Goliath towered over his armor bearer who was standing in front of him. Saul was right; the giant almost appeared twice David's height.

David had once again reached a point of no return. He would leave this battlefield a victor or die trying. His mind, however, downplayed the thought of death. With God Almighty on his side, he wouldn't die! He remembered the lion. Had he been frightened? Sure. As the situation unfolded, David pressed into God's power. He felt that same power surging through his veins. He became aware that he was not alone in his fight against the giant.

No, David realized, *Goliath may be one of, if not the most powerful warrior on the planet, but he doesn't stand a chance against God and His anointed*. A created thing against the Creator was no match—not even close. And yet, here David stood, sun blazing and heart beating out of his chest.

David saw a shimmer of glowing red fire in the giant's bulging eyes as Goliath howled in laughter. It was a sadistic sound—hollow and eerie! David knew this was a very evil man, driven by a force beyond the human realm. Yes, something primal and ancient was driving this man. He realized that now.

Goliath shouted to David, "Am I a dog, that you come at me with sticks?" The Philistine cursed David by his gods. "Come here," he sneered, "and I'll give your flesh to the birds and the wild animals!"

It wasn't time to toy with this killing machine. Goliath was a master manipulator and intimidator, and David would have no part in his shenanigans. *This is no flesh and blood battle*, David reminded himself. *I'm not fighting a human battle here. This is spiritual.*

And with that, he replied to the Philistine, "You come against me with sword and spear and javelin, but I come against you in the name of the Lord Almighty, the God of the armies of Israel, whom you have defied. This day the Lord will deliver you into my hands, and I'll strike you down and cut off your head" (1 Sam 17:45–46).

That was a strange thing to say, David thought. He didn't even have a sword in his possession. And yet, the statement was out there. Beyond his understanding—and by faith—it was out there. There was no turning back.

David felt the host of eyes on his back. He didn't dare turn around, not in the presence of this highly trained warrior. But he felt the stares.

Abner, King Saul, and the commanders of hundreds and thousands, all staring at a young shepherd boy in shepherd's clothing and no sword, a boy nobody had heard of. At that moment, David realized how preposterous he must look. David looked down at himself and then up at the giant. *I must look like a boy, a mere child. But as foolish as I look out here, I've done something no one offered himself to be. I've offered myself as a vessel for God to work through.*

And when David *would* defeat the giant, everyone—including David—would know who defeated the uncircumcised Philistine monster.

David cried all the louder, "And then I will give the dead bodies of your men to the birds and wild animals, and the whole world will know that there is a God in Israel! And everyone assembled here will know that the Lord rescues his people, but not with sword and spear. This is the Lord's battle, and he will give you to us!" (1 Sam 17:46–47).

The giant heaved his head back in laughter. "That's right," David muttered under his breath. "Go ahead and poke your fun at the teenage shepherd boy with no armor and no sword. In your pride, you will fall!"

While the giant was distracted, David reached into his shepherd's bag, took out a stone, and hurled it from his sling. It hit the Philistine square in the forehead. The stone sank in deep, and the man fell on his face to the ground.

A shout erupted from behind him! David turned to the ecstatic throng of Israeli fighters who were wildly cheering. As David ran to his opponent, the armor bearer bolted away. Since he had no sword, David ran over and pulled Goliath's from its sheath, killed him with it, and then cut off his head.

More shouts! More applause! The sound almost rattled David's bones. At the same time, a cry of terror rose from the army of the Philistine camp. David held the head of their champion high in the air and shouted, "Praise the God of Israel! Praise the one and only living God Almighty!"

At once, the Philistine army turned their backs and retreated in terror. They knew it was over. The battle was won. Their champion —and their gods—had been defeated!

DAY 13: SATURDAY
REFLECTIONS FROM THE WEEK

In short, 1 Samuel 17:55–18:6 is a good description of how, overnight, David went from a lowly shepherd to a national celebrity:

> As Saul was watching David go out to fight Goliath, he asked Abner, the general of his army, "Abner, what sort of family does this young fellow come from?" "I really don't know," Abner said. "Well, find out!" the king told him. After David had killed Goliath, Abner brought him to Saul with the Philistine's head still in his hand. "Tell me about your father, my boy," Saul said. And David replied, "His name is Jesse and we live in Bethlehem" (1 Sam 17:55–59).

How interesting. Although David had played the harp on many occasions in the king's presence, these verses prove that Saul had no recollection of the young shepherd. Saul certainly felt better when David played, but didn't acknowledge the source. Why? He spoke one language: war. Now that David had proved himself in a way Saul understood, this was his response:

King Saul now kept David with him and wouldn't let him return home anymore. He was Saul's special assistant, and he always carried out his assignments successfully. So Saul made him commander of his troops, an appointment that was applauded by the army and general public alike (1 Sam 18:4-5).

In one day, at a moment of God's choosing, David, an unknown shepherd from a family nobody knew or cared about, suddenly became the most famous warrior in all Israel. The countless hours of preparation had led him to *this* one defining moment. His brothers were silenced and never heard from again except in genealogical records. Samuel's prophecy was coming to pass. David's time had finally arrived. We see now, had he not been faithful to his father's household and *those few sheep* his brother Eliab spoke of, he would not have encountered the bear or the lion.

The truth is: Compared to a mature male lion or a full-grown bear, Goliath wasn't really a big threat in David's mind. Although big and scary, we can see how David had been thoroughly prepared for the challenge.

Consider this: David passed the bravery test in *private* before he showed his valor in *public*. Some people never reach their defining moment because they can't show their faithfulness when no one is watching and, thus, never rise to their rightful place in the public eye.

David was tested twice in private. He defeated the lion and the bear when no one was watching. Then, God gave him a temporary glimpse by placing him in King Saul's service. His eternal destiny was just around the corner even though David didn't fully understand what God was doing at the time. His destiny was delayed. And as we will find out, there would be further delays. One thing was certain: David was well on his journey and passing tests along the way. There is no more famous story in the Old Testament than David and Goliath. And even though hard times lay ahead for him, his victory over the Philistine champion was never disputed. David's valor (long before he became king) would be talked about from that day on and for countless centuries afterward.

DAY 14: SUNDAY
A CLOSER LOOK AT PSALM 144

One of the things I find fascinating about Scripture is how God seldom does things the same way. His ways are brilliantly creative and mysterious.

When Abraham chose to believe God's promise, he and his wife Sarah were given a son at an age when their bodies were incapable of producing children. After Isaac was born, God asked Abraham to ascend Mount Moriah and slay him on the altar. Abraham obeyed God, but at the last second—just before plunging the dagger—an angel called out to Abraham, and the child was spared. What God asked the patriarch to do has never been asked by anyone again.

The children of Israel were enslaved and then delivered by Moses after God used a series of plagues to move Pharaoh to release them. When the Egyptian army pursued the Israelites, God parted the Red Sea and led them through on dry ground. He then crushed the army which followed hard after them. The way Israel was freed and the way they devastated their oppressors have never been repeated.

Then, there were others like Joshua who was instructed to

encircle the city of Jericho, marching around it seven times, and then shouting, causing the city's walls to fall. And what about Samson? While chained between two pillars, God restored Samson's strength so he could crush the Philistines in one fatal act. Remember Gideon? He defeated an entire Midianite army with three hundred men and no weapons except a torch, a jar, and a trumpet. All these were one-time occurrences.

One of my first tasks as a young pastor was starting a college ministry. During those years, we reached hundreds of college students and young adults. Although we had the typical "church kids" in our group, by and large, the majority were not "churched."

The more I preached to the group, the more I realized I was not speaking their language. Why? I spoke with one very slanted bias: as if they already knew the outcome of the Bible stories I was telling.

At first, it was very frustrating. I had to explain every little detail of the story for them to fully grasp the message. I had not known many were hearing the stories for the first time. Surprisingly, the more I spoke to this group, the more I enjoyed it. In my preparation, I began reading Bible stories in fresh ways, many times pretending I was hearing them for the first time. Most importantly, I read them as if I didn't know the outcome.

David was an incredible forerunner of finding faith during worship. Not only did he do great exploits such as defeat Goliath, but he voiced things about God in a language people had never heard. Through the Psalms, we have the privilege of gazing into the heart of a man who praised God without knowing the outcome of the story.

Although we don't know exactly when it was written, I think the first verse of Psalm 144—"Praise the Lord, who is my Rock. He trains my hands for war"—could have been the prayer of each aforementioned patriarch (i.e., Abraham, Joshua, Samson, and Gideon). It certainly could have fit their dilemmas as well as many situations in David's life.

Consider David's words in Psalm 144 as if you don't know the outcome—that David would defeat Goliath. Consider it before he became king. How about David's praise to God while trying to serve a king whose jealous rage drove him mad or while facing a lion that wanted to tear him limb from limb?

Take a moment and think about your struggles. Then, take your hands and hold them out in front of you (I can imagine David doing this). Now, praise God for training those hands to do great exploits (like conquer giants and persevere in times of difficulty) until you fulfill *your* destiny.

And even though you don't know the outcome because it hasn't happened yet, take a lesson from David who was trained by God Himself to do battle in a way no one had ever before seen. Then, fight with the tactic God gives you. He may ask you to fight *your* giant without a sword but with a slingshot instead. If you're fighting for someone's salvation—a prodigal son or daughter—perhaps, God will lead you to pray for Him to plant someone in your child's path to speak what you cannot. Be obedient to His voice and pray by His direction. God knows the outcome, and, like David, I can assure you, His strategy will yield the best results. As He leads you, I encourage you to praise Him ahead of time—in faith—for the victory!

Week 3
ZERO TO HERO

DAY 15: MONDAY
1 SAMUEL 18:1–4

Shortly after his miraculous victory over Goliath, David was surprised by something quite profound that occurred. The battle over, he was approached by a young man he recognized. He had seen the man on occasion from his harp-playing days in the king's tent. David had liked him from what he knew of him. The young man seemed kind-hearted and appeared to have a good head on his shoulders. His name was Jonathan, and he was the king's son.

David had curiously watched Jonathan during those days in the king's tent. He wanted to see how Jonathan handled the pressure of being the king's son. David was impressed by what he witnessed. He learned it was one thing to be an outsider who earned recognition by performance yet quite another to be recognized by one's association with someone of position or power. He supposed Jonathan must have met many people who said these or similar words—"Oh, you're the king's son. Nice to meet you." David wondered if Jonathan ever wanted to say, "My name is Jonathan—just Jonathan," or was tempted to think, *I'm more than the king's son, for goodness sake!*

Saul had been introducing David to important people after his victory. When the excitement of the day's battle finally died down, David exited the king's tent to gather himself. That was when Jonathan approached him. He heard the familiar voice say, "That was quite a display of valor out there today. I've never seen anything quite like it."

"Thank you," David replied.

"Everybody's talking about it, how it was a great victory and how God was definitely on your—our—side."

David couldn't help but feel the king's son was somehow testing him. He was genuinely warm and friendly. And yet, David felt he was also being sized up. "Yes, I knew God was asking me to fight, and, fortunately, your father gave me permission."

"Yeah, I heard."

"When I saw Goliath and heard what he was saying, it made me so angry. I couldn't believe how he flippantly defied God Almighty and how afraid the army was."

Jonathan listened intently. David could tell Jonathan was taking in his words. But it was true. And, even though Jonathan's father should have taken charge, David couldn't help how it sounded. *Had Jonathan wanted to fight the giant?* David didn't know. *I'm sure the thought must have crossed his mind.* And yet, here they stood—roles reversed in a strange sort of way. As odd as it may have seemed, David sensed Jonathan was okay with the reversal.

"You are a good man," Jonathan said with sincerity in his voice. "I've seen the warrior on the battlefield, but I sense there's more to you than that."

David felt himself draw back, unsure what was happening. It felt almost as if the king's son were giving him his blessing. *His blessing*, David wondered, *his blessing as what? As a welcomed part of the army? Or is it something more?* David wasn't sure, but one thing he knew: Jonathan was sincere, and he appreciated it.

"Thank you. That means a lot, especially coming from the king's son," David said.

Jonathan winced a bit. "Yeah, about that. My dad has his, well, his quirks. He can be," He paused, almost as if he didn't want to continue, but decided he needed to, "well, let's just say he can be somewhat, uh, overbearing and temperamental at times. You'll see." Placing his hand on David's shoulder, he finished, "Well, I just wanted you to know that I'm here—for anything you need."

David looked inquiringly at him. Should he react? Should he tell Jonathan how he played the harp when his dad fell into his fits of depression—or rage? David decided against it; instead, he simply thanked him.

Something happened at that moment. Deep emotion welled up in David's heart for the king's son. It was strange. He loved him for some reason and felt they would be true friends, *Like brothers in arms.* He pondered that idea as he stood there, his mind awash with the exchange with Jonathan. He was amazed that Jonathan didn't appear threatened but seemed genuinely happy for his success. It felt surreal given the response of his actual brothers. They hadn't said a kind word to him. They were silenced, yes. But were they complimentary? Not in the least. "Thank you," David said, almost tearing up. "That means more than you know."

Jonathan

As they talked, Jonathan sensed something in the young shepherd warrior. He barely knew him but identified with the deep inward wound in David. It reminded him of himself. It was a frailty that came from one place—rejection. Jonathan felt it at times and, while talking with David, realized he had no one to confide in. He certainly couldn't share his feelings with his dad.

Jonathan became one in spirit with David, and he loved him as himself.... And Jonathan made a covenant with David because he loved him as himself. Jonathan took off the robe he was wearing and gave it to David, along with his tunic, and even his sword, his bow and his belt (1 Sam 18:1 3-4 NIV).

At last, he had a confidant and trusted friend—maybe even a brother.

DAY 16: TUESDAY
1 SAMUEL 18:5–9

David

David went from a *zero* to a *hero* in a single day. *Shepherd Boy vs. Enemy Giant* was a sensational story and spread throughout the kingdom like wildfire. Slingshot sales went through the roof at local markets as boys of all ages had to have the *David Special,* a.k.a. the *Giant Killer.* It was obvious that God had done a marvelous thing in Israel, but it also appeared that Israel had a new champion.

Before the historic event, David would enter a room quietly, unknown, and unrecognized. Now, everywhere he went, all eyes were on him. People pointed and whispered to each other, and everyone wanted to talk to him. Even the king often called for him, and it was known to all that Saul had himself a new right-hand man.

As Joseph had learned when God promoted him to Pharaoh's palace, David soon discovered that, when one is favored, people notice. People not only saw him differently, but they began to step aside for him. They wanted to hear his thoughts about the kingdom—and they listened. David wasn't used to that, yet it felt good.

David also accepted the king's offer to become his armor bearer but refused to become his son-in-law. The king was hurt and asked, "Why not marry my daughter? You heard about the prize I offered to defeat Goliath."

"Who am I to become your son-in-law?" David reasoned. "I'm just an unknown shepherd from an unknown household. Please honor me by upholding my wishes."

Saul was disappointed, but David's response was good enough for the time being. It appeared King Saul had other plans for David. The king put him in charge of an army and then sent him out to fight. King Saul knew David was brave but wanted to see if he was a good commander.

David did not disappoint. Over the next few years, the Lord was with him, and he never lost a battle. Saul learned that, whenever David was in charge, he need not concern himself with the war. For David, that ended up being a blessing but—ultimately—a curse.

Saul

This is nice, Saul thought. After years of recruiting an army, drawing up battle plans, and fighting war after war, he finally had some relief. Fighting Israel's battles had been exhilarating for the first few years—the dream of any young, aspiring warrior. *But I'm not as young as I used to be*, Saul relented with a sigh. War was tiring—and draining.

Lately, he had stayed back and sent his young star, David, instead. The men were due to return, and a celebration was being held in their honor. As always, the king's presence was required, so Saul rode out to meet them.

The procession had already begun when the king arrived. He wasn't worried. David's being in charge ensured victory. He congratulated some soldiers as he rode by. The music was loud and very joyous, and Saul already knew: *Once again, David has had success!*

"Women came out from among the towns of Israel to meet King Saul with singing and dancing, with joyful song and with timbrels and lyres. As they danced, they sang: 'Saul has slain his thousands, and David his tens of thousands!'" (1 Sam 18:6–7 NIV).

The king scowled and cursed. He "was very angry; this refrain displeased him greatly. 'They have credited David with tens of thousands,' he thought, 'but me with only thousands. What more can he get but the kingdom?' And from that time on, Saul kept a close eye on David" (1 Sam 18:8–9 NIV).

David

David triumphantly returned. All the fanfare was a bit much, but it certainly seemed to mean a great deal to his men. *Let them be celebrated*, he thought. *They deserve it. After all, they fought well.*

Unlike Joseph who was given carte blanche control over all of Egypt's resources, David felt watched—even manipulated at times. It caused him to wonder, *What is it I'm feeling?* It reminded him of something vaguely familiar, almost like being in the presence of —*My brothers*, he realized.

David was scarcely back to his tent when he received word, "The king needs you. Oh, and bring your harp. The king wants you to play for him."

David knew what that meant and gulped. "Tell the king I'll be there shortly," he told the messenger.

Darkness loomed in the air. David felt it. Before he left, he prayed: "The Lord is my light and my salvation—whom shall I fear?

The Lord is the stronghold of my life—of whom shall I be afraid?" (Ps 27:1 NIV).

DAY 17: WEDNESDAY
1 SAMUEL 18:10–11

David had seen Saul's fits of rage before. *What could the king possibly be upset or depressed about?* he questioned. *We were victorious. The Philistines were crushed!*

Deep down David knew. Unlike Joseph, who stayed in Egypt for the remainder of his life, in the ranks of Pharaoh, David wasn't sure how long this would last. The king had manic emotional episodes. The sad part of it all was how it could affect his relationship with Jonathan. David couldn't imagine his life without the king's son. Over time, the two had become like brothers.

David's heart rate elevated as he approached the king's house. His hands were clammy and trembled slightly. The way the king had looked at him upon their return from the battle was unnerving. It made the hair on his neck stand up on end for some reason. Jonathan had been there and acted as a buffer between them. David paused just outside the door and wondered, *Is Jonathan here, now?*

David hoped so, but on entering, not only was Jonathan not there, neither was anyone else. The two men were alone.

"Come in, my son," Saul said. "I've been waiting for you."

My son? David closed the door. It was dark with flickering shadows from several lit candles. The king was sitting—almost sprawled out—on a rug with a troubled look on his face.

"You called for me?" David asked.

"Yes, yes. Please play for me. I always feel—" the king hesitated, appearing to be lost in thought— "well, you know, uplifted when you play."

"What troubles you, my King? God has given us victory over our enemies," David said.

Saul's anger flared, and he muttered something under his breath. David sensed an evil force in the room that made his stomach turn. It was old, ancient, perhaps. Whatever it was, the force seemed to have its grip on the king's mood.

It had been some time since David had worshiped for him. Without a second thought, he headed to his usual place behind the king, as far out of the way as possible, but Saul protested, "No, not behind me. Set up and play over there," he said, pointing to the front-most corner.

David took his harp and started to play with his back to the king but hesitated. He chose to turn and face Saul directly.

David continued to feel very uneasy, but he began playing anyway, closely studying the king. Saul's eyes were closed as he lay his head back.

A little less stressed, David worshiped, and the presence of the evil force or spirit began to dissipate. Its disappearance seemed to light up the room. *Where are the shadows? It seems brighter in here. How strange,* he reflected. And yet, the king still seemed vexed and irritated—noticeably bothered by something. *Is he angry with me?* David couldn't help but wonder. It sure seemed like it. Something about the way he caught King Saul looking at him creeped him out.

Suddenly, the king began speaking—talking very passionately. David kept playing, though. David kept playing, kept worshiping, not allowing the king's action to unsettle him, that is, until he realized what Saul was saying. He almost dropped his harp from shock. *Is he prophesying?*

David wasn't necessarily surprised. He'd heard the stories. "Is Saul among the prophets?" people would say. It was true. David wasn't shocked that Saul was prophesying; rather he was dumbfounded by the words the king was saying: "I have reserved for Myself a man after My own heart to lead My people Israel," Saul cried. "He is better than you, oh King, because he listens to My voice and obeys My commands!"

David couldn't believe his ears, but he calmed himself and played on his instrument. The evil spirit was gone, he knew, and whatever he was hearing came by divine inspiration.

Saul continued, "Through him, through My chosen servant, I will establish My covenant and a lasting dynasty for a thousand generations!"

The king appeared entranced, but it made David feel even more uncomfortable and on guard. Emotions were escalating, and whatever the king was experiencing terrified him.

Abruptly, Saul grabbed a spear beside him, reared back, and thrust it at David. David jumped out of the way and just in the nick of time. With a loud *thud,* the spear came to a halt as it penetrated the wall behind him. "*Grrr!*" the king growled in anger, jumping to his feet.

Fear gripped David, causing him to quickly scurry out the door, forgetting his harp behind him. Servants met him outside and asked, "Is the king okay? Is he hurt?"

"He's fine," David replied, a bit breathless from his near-death experience. "The king is angry, but he's fine." Their hollow stares made him question himself: *What's going on? What have I done wrong?* In that disconcerting moment, David began to question everything.

From inside, Saul's voice bellowed, "I'm sorry, David, my son! Come back!"

But David didn't return to the king's chambers. Instead, he ran in the opposite direction.

DAY 18: THURSDAY
1 SAMUEL 18:10–11

In his lifetime, David had suffered through some restless nights. On this night, however, he felt turmoil that wracked his soul in a way he had never experienced. David shook his head. *What had possessed the king? Why would he want to kill me?*

David lay awake tormented by the very idea that the king had tried to kill him. He tossed and turned so much that he never quite settled himself to sleep. Not long before, he had defeated the giant, and the king had applauded him for it. No, more than that, the king had honored and promoted him throughout all Israel for his victory. *What had changed?* David had done nothing but obey the king's every command. He had risked his life for Saul and had been the king's most devout armor bearer.

Should I tell Jonathan? David pondered before deciding against it. *How could I ever tell my friend what his father tried to do to me? It's best I keep quiet,* he reasoned.

David tried to convince himself the whole thing was an accident. But he knew deep down what Saul had attempted to do. The king had flown off the handle before and thrown things. He had cursed and chewed people out who disappointed him. In matters of war—and life and death—that was to be expected. But this was different. There was no visible trigger.

The longer David lay there, one thing he was sure of: Saul meant to harm him. Why? He didn't know. But from this day forward, David would have to stay on high alert. He continued to stew sleeplessly. He fretted all night long until, at dawn, a messenger came.

"King Saul has requested your presence, David," he said.

David's heart sank. He had no idea how to respond, but he had to say something. "I'll be there shortly," David replied.

"The king said it was urgent," the messenger insisted.

"I understand," David replied and excused himself, returning to his quarters.

What do I do? he prayed, in despair. He had left his harp behind the day before and had no instrument to play. Acapella, David sang a new song unto the Lord. Out of anguish and desperation, he found himself singing, "Let all the faithful pray to You while You may be found. . . . You are my hiding place; You will protect me from trouble and surround me with songs of deliverance" (Ps 32:6–7 NIV).

The words seemed to spring from his lips—*songs of deliverance!* Never had he felt so assured that his worship had the power to deliver him. He had had many brushes with death but never at the hand of his king. He didn't know how to feel about that. And yet, his worship had somehow dramatically deepened. That didn't help him know what to do. So he continued on singing, "I will instruct you and teach you in the way you should go; I will counsel you with My loving eye on you. . . . The Lord's unfailing love surrounds the one who trusts in Him. Rejoice in the Lord and be glad, you righteous; sing, all you who are upright in heart!" (Ps 32:8, 10–11 NIV).

David *did* rejoice, not in his current situation, but in the Lord's power to save him. Before he left to see Saul, he made a conscious decision to trust in God no matter what happened. Even with all that transpired the day before, he knew God would once again help him to approach King Saul with grace and dignity, even honoring him, maybe not for his actions, but certainly for his position.

DAY 19: FRIDAY
1 SAMUEL 18:23

Some distance away from the king's house, David regained his composure. With every step he took, he found strength in the Lord. God was with him; he knew that.

As David approached, the king was outside and saw David coming. David wondered how Saul would conduct himself after the previous night.

To David's surprise, Saul happily greeted him, "David, my son!"

Son? David wondered why the king kept calling him that.

"Walk with me," Saul said. "I have something I need to talk about with you."

"Okay," said David as he allowed the king to lead him.

Servants were busy working around them. David didn't fear—at least not just yet. But given the night before, being in King Saul's presence still felt awkward.

The two men walked in silence for a good while. The sun was out, and birds chirped from the nearby trees. It couldn't have been a more beautiful morning. David was used to the king's mood swings, but his behavior had become increasingly strange. One minute, King

Saul tried to spear him to the wall, and, the next, he happily engaged him in conversation. *Was it his weird conduct that Jonathan wanted to let me know about?*

"I'm sorry for my behavior," Saul broke the silence. "You know how upset I get. It's this war! And it seems endless." The king stopped and stared off into the distance. He continued, "I've been at war for years. And sometimes, I just can't turn it off."

"I don't understand," David said.

"You wouldn't," Saul retorted. "Not until you've walked in my—"

David noticed the king become somewhat irritated. His shoulders tensed, and the veins in his neck bulged. He stopped and placed his massive hand on David's shoulder. King Saul squeezed it so tightly that David winced as pain shot down his arm. David didn't dare react, though.

"Just trust me," the king said, gripping his shoulder even more forcefully, "I've been at war a long time. And, the older a man gets, the more he begins to think about his future—and the legacy he'll leave behind."

"I understand," David said through clenched teeth.

"And that's why I called you here—to talk about something else," the king said, letting David go. Then, oddly, he laughed. "And I don't want you to refuse me this time!"

David had a feeling he knew where the conversation was headed. "That depends, my King. What are you asking?"

"For you to become my son-in-law, of course!" Saul exclaimed. "Take my daughter, Michal, as your wife, and you will become a part of my family." The king's tone was serious at this point. The cadence of his words changed; it slowed down as if he wanted David not to miss a word of what he was saying. "As you saw last night—a man can only be refused for so long."

David looked right into Saul's eyes and held his ground. "Oh, King, as tempting as that is," he said, "do you think it is a small matter to become the king's son-in-law? I'm only a poor man and little known" (1 Sam 18:23 NIV).

Saul's face tensed in obvious disappointment. "I only hope you will think about my offer."

"I will," David said. "Is that all the King wanted from your servant?"

"Yes. You can go," he answered.

David had hoped for resolution or even answers concerning the king's actions. Instead, as he returned home, he felt trapped. Nothing was resolved, and he couldn't experience the freedom and rest that accompany a problem solved. Later, a few of the king's advisers met with him and encouraged him to accept the king's offer.

David wanted to say, "Is this your advice or the king's," but he didn't. Instead, he deflected, "I come from a poor household. How could I pay the bride price for the daughter of a king?"

Saul sent this reply to David, "Tell the son of Jesse I will only accept the price of a hundred Philistine foreskins to take revenge on my enemies."

To rid himself of his enemies—or rid himself of me? David wondered. He couldn't be sure. After this challenge, however, David was pleased to become the king's son-in-law and didn't bring back one hundred foreskins—but two hundred. Saul then gave him his daughter, Michal, in marriage.

It's done! David was relieved. *I'm officially a part of the king's family.* He and Jonathan were now brothers by marriage. David was sure becoming the king's son-in-law would extinguish Saul's ill feeling toward him. *I'm no threat anymore*, he concluded. *My troubles are over, and I can get on with my life.*

David soon found out, however, that Saul's wrath seemed inflamed even more. His troubles had just begun.

DAY 20: SATURDAY
REFLECTIONS FROM THE WEEK

Have you ever felt like you had to tiptoe around someone —always afraid to say the wrong thing? Has your every move come under the critical observation of another? Perhaps, you've had a boss who scrutinized how you did your job or interacted with others. Of course, it would be hard to imagine your boss throwing a spear at you, but still I think you can in some way relate to David's experience.

Imagine, if you will, being David and having a crazed person terrorize you. It seemed, no matter how much success he had, David couldn't win.

I remember meeting a boat mechanic who, from the time I met him, always said, "God has it out for me!" In his case, I had a hard time believing he knew God. Given his appearance and his attitude, it was understandable how bad choices led to less than desirable results.

David, on the other hand, had done nothing wrong, yet he was being punished. With all the spear throwing and intimidating conversations, David maintained a good attitude. How do I know this? Let's look at Saul's actions in 1 Samuel 18:11. It says, "Saul hurled the spear for he thought, 'I will pin David to the wall.' But David escaped from his presence twice" (NASB).

Wait a second. Did you catch that? Saul tried to pin David to the wall not once—but *twice*. What kind of a man returns to his post after almost being killed at the hand of a king? David was either crazy or had a crazy trust in his God. There was no way around it; David was in a tough position. And that can be frustrating, even for a man after God's own heart.

I am reminded of what Elijah told his young apprentice when Elisha asked for a double portion of his master's anointing. "'You have asked a difficult thing,' Elijah replied. 'If you see me when I am taken from you, then you will get your request. But if not, then you won't'" (2 Kgs 2:10).

Based on his master's answer, there were a couple of obvious assumptions Elisha must have made: (1) Elijah would be taken from him at some point, and (2) Elisha knew he must stick close to his master at all times. Imagine waking up every day wondering if this were the day your master would be taken from you. What pressure and poise Elisha must have had. There were no days off. Elisha constantly stuck to Elijah's side, ever being on guard, watching, patiently waiting, and questioning, *Is this the day? Is this the hour? Is this the moment?*

When the day finally came, sure enough, Elijah tested his young apprentice by taking an unexpected journey. First, they went to Gilgal where Elijah instructed him to wait. "No sir," Elisha demanded, "I'm not going to leave you." On three different occasions, Elijah tried to sway him to stay (Gilgal, Bethel, and Jericho), but Elisha refused (see 2 Kgs 2:1–10).

In David's case, there was no way around it. As Elisha found out, walking out the plan of God was hard. It was tiring, and it took discipline. Yet, David continued to exercise extreme caution around

King Saul. He was careful to keep the king at a safe distance, at least as much as was possible.

Don't be misled by the slew of well-meaning teachers and preachers who assert that God's promise of "abundant life" (John 10:10) equates to an "easy life." Even though Matthew 11:30 describes God's load as easy and His burden as light, don't miss the analogy: two oxen plowing a load—together. It's work. It requires sweat. It requires faith and perseverance. And it means submission to the yoke.

The same God who promised abundant life also promised, "Yes, and everyone who wants to live a godly life in Christ Jesus will suffer persecution" (2 Tim 3:12). David learned there were hardships to endure and difficulties to face. And as they came, he also learned how to take the burdens of them all to God. He was anointed and favored to do great exploits, and, like Elijah, God's response to him was, "You have asked a difficult thing." Sometimes that's the only answer: To reach your divine destiny, it's going to be *difficult*.

Perhaps, it was in such perilous times that David cried out as in Psalm 27:1:

> The Lord is my light and my salvation—so why should I be afraid?
> The Lord is my fortress, protecting me from danger, so why should I tremble?

DAY 21: SUNDAY
A CLOSER LOOK AT PSALM 27

It is encouraging to know that such an incredible man (whose life is celebrated more than any other in Scripture besides Jesus) had moments of dealing with agony, fear, and disappointment. As I read Psalm 27:1, I should remember that David was crying out to God in creative nuances never before heard.

I can imagine David awaking from sleep out in the open plain. He rubs the sleep from his eyes, maybe washing his face in a creek, and then finds a place on some rock as the sun is rising. As the light emerges, it slowly illuminates the enemy camp where he and his men are about to wage war. David strums a few strings on his harp, and sings, "The Lord is my light, and my salvation. Whom then shall I fear?"

I don't think I've ever sung from a place where life or death hung in the balance—a place where my very life was threatened by evil forces intent on stabbing me to death with a sword or shooting me with an arrow. I've also never had my boss chuck a spear at me in a jealous rage.

David goes on to talk about the situation that is brewing. It starts out with enemies attacking, invading his territory, and escalates into a full-blown war. Surprisingly, he doesn't cry out for victory. Instead, maybe sitting on a rock overlooking the situation, he pens one of his more famous sayings: "One thing I ask from the Lord, this only do I seek: that I may dwell in the house of the Lord all the days of my life, to gaze on the beauty of the Lord and to seek Him in His temple" (Ps 27:4 NIV).

Huh? Really, David? Surrounded by evil and wicked men out to destroy you, and that's the *one thing* you want right now? Fascinating approach.

David had found the answer to any problem or any situation: gazing at the beauty of the Lord in His holy temple. Wait a minute. There was no temple back then. In fact, there wasn't even a tabernacle in his day. When the ark of the covenant came back to Jerusalem, David had to pitch a tent for it; it was a makeshift tabernacle without the wall leading to the most holy place. The temple David must have been referring to was whatever place (whatever rock, tree, mountain, tent, etc.) he found to seek God's face.

When I read David's famous "One Thing" passage, I find myself thinking of Mary and Martha in the presence of Jesus. Martha was busy trying to serve the Lord while Mary was contently nestled at His feet. It makes me wonder if she was captured with the same overwhelming awe and wonder David was: gazing at the beauty of the Lord.

Martha got annoyed with Mary, however, because Martha had to do all the work alone. It makes me think of my own shortcomings— always working, writing, studying, or even ministering to people. Though none of these things are bad, it's my always being busy that's the issue. The only problem for Martha was that the Son of God and second person of the Holy Trinity—God Almighty—was in her home.

Jesus tells Mary's sister, "Martha, Martha, you are anxious and troubled about many things" (Luke 10:41). Isn't it just like Jesus to call our distractions for what they really are—*trouble*. I don't know about you, but I tend to find myself troubled about many things much of the time. Jesus went on to tell Martha what David spoke of in Psalm 27. Jesus said, "There is *only one thing* worth being concerned about. Mary has discovered it, and it will not be taken away from her" (Luke 10:42 emphasis mine).

David does it again. Eight hundred years before Jesus walked the earth in human form, David conveys the heart of God. In the middle of having spears thrown at him, being scrutinized, and fighting bloody battles, David correctly chooses. Maybe that's why in the next breath he pens, "For in the *day of trouble* he will keep me safe in his dwelling; he will hide me in the shelter of his sacred tent and set me high upon a rock" (Ps 27:5 emphasis mine).

I can picture David sprawled out on a rock, worshiping the Lord. Who knows, it could have been hours after his near-death worship session with King Saul. Instead of being troubled as Martha was and as we so often are, David, in his *day of trouble,* chooses wisely: David sits at the Lord's feet, gazing upon the Lord's beauty.

Are you troubled about many things? Take some time to unplug from the distractions. Read and meditate on Psalm 27:1–5 and then worship the Lord knowing He will deliver you in *your* day of trouble:

> The Lord is my light and my salvation—whom shall I fear? The Lord is the stronghold of my life—of whom shall I be afraid? When the wicked advance against me to devour me, it is my enemies and my foes who will stumble and fall. Though an army besiege me, my heart will not fear; though war break out against me, even then I will be confident. One thing I ask from the Lord, this only do I seek: that I may dwell in the house of the Lord all the days of my life, to gaze on the beauty of the Lord and to seek

Him in His temple. For in the day of trouble He will keep me safe in His dwelling; He will hide me in the shelter of His sacred tent and set me high upon a rock (Ps 27:1–5 NIV).

Week 4
FRIEND OR FOE?

DAY 22: MONDAY
1 SAMUEL 18:28–30; 19:1–3

Jonathan

"Come here, my boy," Saul said to his eldest son. "We need to talk about a real threat."

Jonathan thought he knew what was coming next: *Dad must have heard some intel on the Philistines' latest movements.* He was in the habit of sending either Jonathan or David to meet them head on or cut them off before they crossed Israeli lines.

"Yes, Dad. What can I do? Are the Philistines on the move again?"

"No, no," Saul replied, scowling. "This has nothing to do with those heathen dogs."

"Oh?"

Saul stroked his chin. "This matter is of a more sensitive nature," the king told his son. "The threat is not outside the camp but within."

Jonathan, with his eyebrow raised, was suddenly alarmed. *Is there a spy? Has a mole infiltrated our ranks?* His curiosity and eagerness to know set him on ready. "Do tell, Father. And I'd be happy to deal with the matter swiftly—and quietly," Jonathan said with a sly look.

"Well, I can tell you, if the matter is not dealt with as you say, 'swiftly and quietly,' the ramifications could be catastrophic for our family—and for the nation."

"What are you talking about, Dad?" he blurted. "Stop beating around the bush and tell me what's going on!"

Saul couldn't help but react to his son's impatient ignorance. "I'm talking about your future crown, Jonathan!" Saul exploded, "As long as David is around, your—our—future will never be secure! You must know that, don't you? You must have seen how he's stolen the heart of all those around him."

Jonathan was stunned. He stammered, "But Dad, uh, you don't—I mean—there's no reason to worry about David. He's done nothing but good. He's loyal to you and to the kingdom. And every task he's given—"

"He must die!" Saul cut him off mid-sentence. "I'm telling you, we must find a way to discard the son of Jesse before he steals your throne!"

Jonathan knew his dad's tone. It was useless to argue with him once he used *that* tone. In his current state of mind, the king had made his decision, and nothing Jonathan could say would talk him out of it. He did have a choice to make—well two, actually. The first was easy, and he did it right away.

"I won't be a part of this, Dad!" Jonathan said, disgusted, and walked off. Saul didn't come after him.

The second choice was more difficult. Not, *Should I tell David?* but rather, because David was in danger: *How should I break the news to my brother?*

Jonathan was too afraid to wait. He had seen the look in his father's eyes before. Once Saul set his mind to do something, he saw it through, that is, unless Jonathan intervened, which Jonathan was determined to do. With haste, Jonathan asked some soldiers in David's ranks, "Where is your master? I need to see him right away."

When Jonathan learned of David's whereabouts, he went to meet David. "And Jonathan told David, 'Saul my father seeks to kill you. Therefore be on your guard in the morning. Stay in a secret place and hide yourself. And I will go out and stand beside my father in the field where you are, and I will speak to my father about you. And if I learn anything I will tell you'" (1 Sam 19:1–3).

David thanked Jonathan and did as he instructed.

On his way home, Jonathan had a strange thought that deeply troubled him. *It appears I am the mole among the ranks. I am the spy.* He had never felt so torn in his life—on the one hand loyalty to his father, on the other to his friend and brother. It was all too much to handle at that moment. He committed himself to figuring out what to do, *In the morning, I will take care of the matter.*

DAY 23: TUESDAY
1 SAMUEL 19:4–6, 9–12

The next morning as Jonathan and his father were talking together, Jonathan did his best to defend his friend. "What has David ever done to harm you?" Jonathan argued. "From where I'm standing, he's done nothing but good. Remember how he defeated Goliath and brought great victory to Israel? You weren't complaining then."

Saul stroked his chin, listening intently to his eldest son.

"Besides, what benefit is there in killing an innocent man?"

Finally, Saul agreed and vowed, "As the Lord lives, he shall not be killed" (1 Sam 19:6).

David

David waited patiently in hiding. What a peculiar circumstance in which to find himself: the king's son-in-law and general of Israel's army hiding like a coward. A knock came to the door that caused David to jump. *Are the king's men at my door? Is it a messenger? Or has Jonathan returned?* Putting his questions aside, David opened the door to see his friend standing there. The two men embraced. "I'm glad it's you," David said, a bit relieved.

"I have wonderful news," Jonathan announced. "I talked to the king, and he has changed his mind. He no longer means to harm you. In fact, he took an oath not to hurt you."

"That's great," David said, trying to sound convincing. *Should I tell Jonathan about the two times his father tried to pin me to the wall while playing my harp?* He thought not. Then, he said, "It's done, and I have nothing to worry about—thanks to you."

"I'm glad I could help," Jonathan said, his face showing his delight.

David looked into the eyes of his friend, and he knew Jonathan thought it was over. Done. Resolved.

Maybe it is? David hoped. They didn't have much time to celebrate as a messenger arrived: "War is upon us. The Philistines have attacked, and you are both summoned to the frontlines."

With confidence, David marched out to meet the Philistines and slaughtered a great number of them. It was such a one-sided victory that, not only did the Philistines suffer many casualties, but they were sent running away in fear. The war was over, and David had triumphed once more.

Saul

Saul opened up the local newspaper while feasting at his table. With all the victories lately, surely he had received some good press. Saul read the reports and then slammed his fist down on the table, spilling his drink. "Aargh!" he grunted. Not one word was spoken about his son Jonathan. And very little was said about him. All he heard anymore was, "David did *this*," and, "David did *that*."

Saul turned to one of his aids. "Where is David? Get him in here! I need him—now! And tell him to bring his harp!"

The words he had spoken to his son Jonathan weighed heavily on his mind. *How can I keep my word to my son?* he pondered. *The son of Jesse must die. Jonathan is a boy and doesn't understand such matters. Yes, he is not thinking clearly because his friendship has clouded his judgment.*

Saul was confident. He knew what he must do. Because of Jonathan's affection for David, Jonathan would never have the courage to do what needed to be done. Only a father with his son's best interest—and the interest of the kingdom—would have the courage to do so.

David

David arrived and began to worship the Lord in the presence of the king. His fear of death had somewhat diminished since Jonathan pleaded his case. *Oh, Jonathan, my brother. You are my greatest ally*, David thought, relieved. In many ways, David felt the king's son was his *only* ally. The more press he had received, the more Saul's advisors seemed standoffish. And the more alienated he felt, the more the need to cry out in worship. Even in the king's presence, he had to cry out with sincerity of heart: "Oh Lord, why do You stand so far away? Why do You hide when I am in trouble? The wicked arrogantly hunt down the poor. Let them be caught in the evil they plan for others" (Ps 10:1-2 NIV).

Have I said too much, David wondered, seemingly lost in thought. The king was occupied—oblivious. David continued: "They think, 'Nothing bad will ever happen to us! We will be free of trouble forever!' Their mouths are full of cursing, lies, and threats. Trouble and evil are on the tips of their tongues" (Ps 10:6).

Who am I talking about, David pondered. *Who are the wicked—the Philistines, or someone else?* He had always had faith in the king and Israel's leadership. He had always felt loyal to the kingdom, but lately, David struggled to get behind their initiatives. He could no longer clearly see whether they were fighting the Lord's battles or the king's? And during worship, a compelling thought gripped him: "The Lord is King forever and ever! The godless . . . will vanish from the land. Lord, You know the hopes of the helpless. Surely You will hear their cries and comfort them" (Ps 10:16–17).

Yes, the Lord is King, David concluded. *The Lord will deal with the wicked and will repay their wrongdoing against the innocent—against me.*

King Saul seemed to react and snap out of his usual trance. "With spear in hand, the tormenting spirit from the Lord suddenly came upon him again. As David played his harp, Saul hurled his spear at David. But David dodged out of the way, and leaving the spear stuck in the wall, he fled and escaped into the night" (1 Sam 19:9–10).

For the third time, David escaped the spear of Saul's anger. And after the third time, David knew he must escape for good, or else he would be killed by the king's hand.

> Saul sent men to David's house to watch it and to kill him in the morning. But Michal, David's wife, warned him, "If you don't run for your life tonight, tomorrow you'll be killed." So Michal let David down through a window, and he fled and escaped (1 Sam 19:11–12 NIV).

DAY 24: WEDNESDAY
1 SAMUEL 19:14–24

Saul sent the men to capture David at his home, but Michal covered for him, saying "He's fallen ill."

Saul was suspicious of his daughter's ploy and sent the men back. "Drag the son of Jesse out of his bed if you have to so that I can kill him."

When the men entered David's room all they found was an idol in the bed, and at the head was some goats' hair.

Saul was furious with his daughter. "How could you deceive me like this and let my enemy get away?"

Michal lied, "He said to me, 'Let me get away. Why should I kill you?'"

Saul

Disgusted, Saul confined his daughter to the house and posted guards before returning home. The men with him did their best to comfort the king, but he was not in a consoling mood. Yet again, David had slipped through his fingers.

"Everyone is against me!" Saul yelled. "Even my own daughter is vouching for the son of Jesse."

One of his aides spoke up. "My King, I don't think Michal would—"

"Shut-up!" Saul silenced him. "I don't want excuses. I want to know where David has gone. Can anyone tell me?"

All his aides looked at each other with unease.

"Go find him!" the king commanded and shooed them away. Just before they made their exit, he yelled to them, "And make sure Jonathan doesn't know where you're going—understand?"

They gave a militant nod and swiftly left Saul's presence.

Retreating into his house, Saul paced the floor of his chambers. It was getting dark. He was tired—and hungry. After calling for food, he relieved himself and drank some wine to relax. In time, his anger subsided, but not before he threw a few things. They shattered with a loud *crash!* A servant started to enter but decided against it, closing the door after seeing the king's mood. Saul glared at the door and set his goblet down. His hand was trembling, and the goblet toppled over. The blood-red liquid poured across the table. *If only it was David's blood!*

Inwardly, Saul fumed at his daughter. Was she lying? Was she covering for him? *Of course, she is. She loves him.*

Saul plopped down on his bed—deflated. How could he blame her? "Yes, everyone is against me," he moaned before laying down and drifting off to sleep. It wasn't a peaceful sleep. As usual, Saul's dreams were plagued by nightmares.

Later, word was delivered to Saul that David was in Naioth at Ramah. He was quick to send his men to capture his son-in-law, but they soon proved of no help to the king as they began prophesying after they came upon Samuel and his group of prophets. Saul was told about it, so he sent more men, who also began prophesying when they came upon the spectacle. He sent a third group of men, and the Spirit of God came upon them, and they started prophesying.

That was it! King Saul, himself, left to find David. "But the Spirit of God came even on him, and he walked along prophesying until he came to Naioth. He stripped off his garments, and he too prophesied in Samuel's presence. He lay naked all that day and all that night. This is why people say, 'Is Saul also among the prophets?'" (1 Sam 19:19–24 NIV).

As Saul lay there, debased and naked, he couldn't make sense of all that had happened. *Why am I prophesying?* he questioned. The answer was always the same. *Because God has left you and given His favor to another.* Sometimes, his prophecies declared victory, but it wasn't on his behalf. God had left him. He felt torn—trapped. Trying to fight the Lord's battles without the Lord's help seemed impossible and the outcome unpredictable. Most of the time he just guessed what to do. And yet, he lingered on: *Fighting—always fighting to get ahead.*

Before dressing himself and preparing to leave, he muttered through pursed lips, "Yes, everyone is against me—even the Lord."

DAY 25: THURSDAY
1 SAMUEL 20:1–23

Jonathan

David didn't look well. He was pale and as haggard as Jonathan had seen.

"What's wrong?"

"It's your father. He's bent on killing me!" David claimed.

"That can't be," Jonathan protested. "He would never do something like this without telling me."

David wouldn't let up. "I promise you, I'm only a step away from death."

Jonathan didn't want to believe it. The more he listened and reflected on Saul's previous actions, the more he realized it wasn't inconceivable that, because of their friendship, Saul might hide something like this from him. Jonathan did want to help his friend. "Tell me what I can do?"

"I'm going to pretend to take a trip to Bethlehem instead of going to the king's dinner the next few days. If your father loses his temper when I'm not there, you'll know something's up."

"Okay," Jonathan agreed. "Tomorrow, I'll do just as you said. Hide in the field by the stone pile. If my father is bent on harming you, I'll shoot an arrow past you. If not, I'll come and get you, and we'll return together."

"I'm sorry it's come to this," David replied.

"No, I'm sorry, sorry for my father's anger. I tried to warn you about it, remember?"

"I know."

David

David hated his current state. Once again, he stood between Saul and Jonathan. *How do I keep ending up between these two? Between a father and his son? Between my king and my friend?*

He tried not to be skeptical. He believed his friend was sincerely looking out for him and knew Jonathan would never betray him. Of that, he was convinced, especially after their last conversation. But David had to be careful. He needed to find a place to go where he wouldn't be recognized. He couldn't go home. He couldn't go to the priest. All he could do was hide out, as instructed, in this remote field. After all, David didn't mind being in the field. He was used to sleeping outdoors in less than desirable conditions. He didn't dare make a fire, though. That would draw too much attention.

No, there was nothing to do but wait. Even with the successes David had achieved in battle, the waiting seemed never to end. It was frustrating. He bowed his head and prayed, "Let all that I am wait quietly before God, for my hope is in Him. He alone is my rock and my salvation, my fortress where I will not be shaken" (Ps 62:5–6).

The story of Esther seemed to surface in his mind. He remembered how Esther had been coerced by her Uncle Mordecai to enter the king's chamber unannounced. It was a risky move, and Esther was hesitant. David thought about his friend. He realized his life lay in the balance, dependent upon how the king reacted to Jonathan.

There was a turning point in Esther's journey, he remembered. *She told her uncle to ask people to fast and pray for three days on her behalf. Should I fast and pray?* David wondered. He marveled at the way God worked during those three days. As he recalled, King Ahasuerus couldn't sleep and was read the book of deeds as a sleep aid. Low and behold, Mordecai was mentioned. The king, realizing Mordecai had not been recognized for his honorable past actions, gave orders to Haman that, in the end, resulted in Haman's demise. And all that happened during three days of fasting.

David once again prayed fervently, "Oh, Lord, over the next three days, open the eyes of my friend Jonathan. Show him the truth of his father's intentions concerning me. Do as You did for Esther and spare my life!"

DAY 26: FRIDAY
1 SAMUEL 20:24–34, 41–42

Jonathan

While David hid in the field, Jonathan acted as normal as possible. He ate at his father's table as usual. Even though David's seat was empty, Saul said nothing the first day. By the second day, however, his father took notice. "Where's David?" Saul asked him.

"I gave him permission to attend a family sacrifice in Bethlehem," Jonathan replied.

Saul boiled with rage at Jonathan. "You stupid son of a whore!" he swore at him. "Do you think I don't know that you want him to be king in your place, shaming yourself and your mother? As long as that son of Jesse is alive, you'll never be king. Now go and get him so I can kill him!" (1 Sam 20:30–31).

Jonathan's heart sank. "I don't understand. Why does he need to die?" he pleaded, in a disappointed tone. "He's done nothing wrong —only supported you."

Saul came unglued and cursed all the more.

"I'm not hungry," Jonathan exclaimed, pushing back from the table. He was angry—yes—but more crushed by his father's shameful attitude toward his friend.

As he left, his father went ballistic, hauled back, and threw his spear at him. "Get out of my sight!" Saul cried.

Upon dodging his dad's spear, Jonathan left the house. It was only a half-hearted throw. He knew his father would never actually hurt him. *Or would he? Had David been right all along?* Jonathan had often seen his father's rage but never like this. And never with the intent to hurt him.

Jonathan gathered himself outside the banquet hall and then walked slowly down the road to clear his head. He felt sad. He felt embarrassed for his father's actions. And at that moment, he realized: *My father has lost it—really lost it!* His father was not himself, not nearly the man Jonathan thought he was.

Maybe that's what drew Jonathan to David. He thought back to the young shepherd boy he had met after defeating Goliath. There was something about him, something different that he couldn't put his finger on. The more he thought about it, the more he realized, *Whatever David has, my father obviously doesn't.*

Jonathan hung his head, not because he dreaded facing David, but because he dreaded what David would do. *He's leaving*, Jonathan sighed, *and never coming back*. For a brief second, he thought of going with him but knew that would never work. His place was here. *With my crazy father.*

As much as he hated him right now, as his firstborn son, he would never leave Saul's side.

Jonathan knew what he had to do and knew he must quickly do it. Being meticulously careful, he made sure he wasn't followed by any of his father's spies. He slipped away to the field where David was waiting.

"David came out from where he had been hiding near the stone pile. Then David bowed three times to Jonathan with his face to the ground. Both were in tears as they embraced each other and said good-bye, especially David" (1 Sam 20:41).

DAY 27: SATURDAY
REFLECTIONS FROM THE WEEK

If I were to title this week's reflections, I would call them, "Death of a Dream." Based on David's experiences in our reading this week, we could conclude that his dreams were officially over. As much as he had hoped to be embraced by Saul and the current leadership, he wasn't. His performance didn't cause them to reject him. His destiny required it. And that destiny could be achieved no other way than by his being refined by the fire of rejection.

In Week 1, not only did we address David's upbringing, but we also discussed the refinement process described by Malachi as a *refiner's fire*. You may remember how difficult a process refinement can be, using extreme heat to remove impurities.

In Week 1, I purposefully didn't mention a second refining process required before gold is considered 100 percent pure (24 karats). It wasn't as pertinent then as it is now in David's journey when his dreams are obliterated.

The first refining process called *smelting* happens rather easily. Rocks and dirt, along with other insignificant alloys, such as copper, nickel, or iron, come out quickly. You heat up the gold until it is hot, and the impurities separate themselves.

The second refining process, which takes place later, is much more difficult. The fire is heated up much hotter before other metals begin to separate from the gold. When the fire is at its hottest, the refiner takes the gold through an intricate process, adding borax and soda ash to separate the most difficult elements. Can you guess what the most difficult element to remove is? It's silver.

Why is silver so difficult to remove? It's simple: Silver is also a precious metal and holds its own weight and beauty. It is precious and valuable though not as precious and as valuable as gold. It isn't worth as much, nor as sought after.

I can relate to David's journey because, early in ministry—for the better part of fifteen years—I was extremely successful. It seemed everything I did was met with favor and prosperity. Don't get me wrong. It wasn't easy. I went through the fire, yet I always triumphed.

God dealt with me on character flaws, challenging me to change, and I responded. He refined my spiritual character by burning away things like pride, lust, and difficulty submitting to leadership. He helped me develop spiritual disciplines by burning away laziness, self-centeredness, and poor time management. During those years, God birthed in me a love for people by burning away self-promotion and a host of other meaningless ambitions. Although hard, I embraced the process, and that got me through the first decade and a half of ministry.

The second refining process, however, was much different. I understand now what the statement, "Good is the biggest enemy of the great," really means. As David learned, the second refining process is where God buries *our* dreams to resurrect *His* dreams. This death by fire is a lesson many struggle to learn. They are comfortable with the good and unwilling to move on to the great. Perhaps, a better way to say it is: They are unwilling to die to the good for God to resurrect the great.

A few years ago, when God began to stir my heart back toward worship, missions, and the greater body of Christ, I remember thinking: *This can't possibly be right. I'm here planting a church, and those things are just distractions.* Deep down, however, I had this sense I was created for something more.

The silver in me said, "You're doing an adequate job. And if you try harder, you'll learn to preach good sermons, run good church services, and plan good outreaches. Your church will grow, and then you'll be happy—and fulfilled!"

The gold in me said, "You can sound a call to start a worship movement that reaches a generation. You can fuel and equip a generation of worshipers to infiltrate the nations. You can sound an alarm that will inspire others to write songs, author books, make movies, and create sound bites that preach Jesus to the masses." I followed that calling, and it has led me to the far reaches of the world.

Joseph experienced the refining process. The silver in him could have been satisfied with having charge over Potiphar's house. But God saw the bigger picture; God saw the gold within him. Thus, God, in His wisdom, allowed Potiphar's wife to take notice of the handsome young man. Being falsely accused led Joseph through the second crucible of refinement to remove the silver, leading him toward the gold where God would place him over Egypt and allow him to save his entire family (see Gen 37–50).

After David killed Goliath and became a household name, I'm sure he assumed becoming king was inevitable. He was Saul's armor bearer, a successful military commander, and the king's son-in-law, highly respected by all. Even Jonathan, the king's son (and next in line) hinted at conceding his throne, admitting, "You're probably going to be the next king after my father—not me." Only a few years after defeating Goliath, everything seemed to be lining up, and David probably thought his ascension to the throne would be smooth sailing from there.

God assessed the situation and implemented phase two of the refinement process, where Saul's jealous anger banished David from the kingdom. God looked at David's life and thought: *There's gold in them there hills but not with all that silver. Time to dig it out.*

What silver are you holding on to? What refinement process have you been resisting? Have you encountered the death of a dream? If you have, know that, as Joseph and David encountered, God is replacing the good with the great. He's burning away the silver and leading you forward to pure gold.

DAY 28: SUNDAY
A CLOSER LOOK AT PSALM 62

Have you heard the expression, "Good things come to those who wait"? David experienced the truth of the adage.

Throughout David's journey, we witness a cycle of his rising up in hope only to be disappointed by circumstances or the actions of others. Time after time, no matter what he did, he couldn't seem to get ahead. In fact, it almost appeared the better he did, the worse he ended up. No doubt, it was frustrating him.

In Psalm 62, for the first time, he identified his lot in life. He said, "I wait quietly before God, for my victory comes from Him. . . Let all that I am wait quietly before God, for my hope is in Him" (vv 1, 6).

David came to realize, *I'm playing the waiting game here.* And he also realized that it was God on whom he was waiting. He postured himself to wait for his only hope of victory: when God would show up and defend him. You notice each of the three times Saul tried to pin him to the wall, David didn't defend himself. He didn't lead a revolt or find a lawyer to plead his case. His only chance was telling the king's son, Jonathan. And even when Jonathan didn't believe him, David didn't get angry at him or lash out. Instead, he waited patiently for God to open Jonathan's eyes to the king's folly.

Maybe that's why David chose to wait *quietly* before God. Defending himself by making a loud fuss or losing his temper wouldn't have done anything but make the situation worse, so he remained silent. He was being falsely accused, his name was being slandered and dragged through the mud, yet he waited quietly and patiently before God, for his hope was in Him. Does David's silent response remind you of anyone else? Jesus "was silent and made no reply" when He stood before the high priest (see Mark 14:60–61).

How many times do we feel the need to speak up when we are treated unfairly? I know I often do. I'm so quick to plead my case. As much as I love democracy, there are certainly downfalls to my upbringing. *Why would you say that?* you may wonder. It's simple: Those who grew up in a democracy tend to live with a democratic mindset, which says: "I have a God-given right to vote and have a voice. And, most of all, I must be given the chance to defend myself and be treated fairly."

I'm sorry to say that the Bible is not based on democracy but on Kingdom principles. I admit that having lived in and loving the U.S.A., it is hard for me to understand Kingdom principles after having been ingrained with a democratic mindset. What David, and, for that matter, Jesus demonstrated during their lifetimes were principles based on Kingdom living. And Kingdom principles say the opposite: "I don't always have a right to vote on the matter, have a voice in the matter, have the chance to retaliate or defend myself, or be treated fairly." *Ouch!* I'll be the first one to admit how wrong that sits with me. And yet, that was the position David and Jesus took.

Have you been defending yourself instead of letting God defend you? Have you been speaking up and throwing temper tantrums, demanding your "God-given," democratic rights?

Both David and Jesus were acquainted with the Kingdom ideal to wait quietly and saying nothing. It comes from Romans 12:19 which quotes a passage from Deuteronomy: "Dearly beloved, avenge not yourselves . . . for it is written, 'Vengeance is Mine; I will repay, says the Lord'" (KJV).

Our job is not to defend ourselves but rather, quietly and patiently, wait upon the Lord. Read this Psalm of David and make it your prayer:

> I wait quietly before God, for my victory comes from Him. He alone is my rock and my salvation, my fortress where I will never be shaken. . . . Let all that I am wait quietly before God, for my hope is in Him. He alone is my rock and my salvation, my fortress where I will not be shaken. My victory and honor come from God alone. He is my refuge, a rock where no enemy can reach me. O my people, trust in Him at all times. Pour out your heart to Him, for God is our refuge (Ps 62:1–2, 5–8).

WEEK 5
OUTLAW ON THE RUN

DAY 29: MONDAY
1 SAMUEL 20:42; 21:1

David

As the two friends parted, Jonathan said to David, "Go in peace, for we have sworn loyalty to each other in the Lord's name. The Lord is the witness of a bond between us and our children forever" (1 Sam 20:42).

After leaving Jonathan's presence in tears, David couldn't help but deliberate about where he should go. Obviously, he couldn't go home. The last thing he wanted to do was put his house in jeopardy. Of course, his wife, Michal, was Saul's daughter, and there was no way Saul would harm his own little girl. *Or would he?* David began to question, *Was the king that crazy? Would he use her to get to me?* For a moment, David hesitated. *Should I go back for her?*

After much turmoil, David resolved not to return. Yes, Saul had lost his mind, but certainly not to that extent. Then, there was Michal. *Would she even leave the kingdom to become*—the thought hit the son of Jesse between the eyes: *I'm now an outlaw! I couldn't go back, even if I wanted to.* The question again befuddled David's mind: *So where should I go?*

Taking one step at a time, David plodded on. Right foot. Left foot. Right. Left. This seemed to be the longest and hardest walk of his life. He thought about his father, mother, and brothers at home. Now that he was on the run, anywhere he went was not only unsafe but would also place those he loved in danger. From what it appeared, King Saul would stop at nothing until David was finished —until he was dead. Each step was met with fresh tears now that he was estranged from his wife, separated from his family, and alienated from his one friend and ally.

Leaving his beloved Jonathan far behind, David headed in the opposite direction toward the one place he was sure to find refuge, if even for a short time. It was a familiar place where he had often prayed, sought God, and inquired of the Lord for victory over his enemies. Up to this point, the Lord had always spoken favorably to David through the priest, Ahimelech. And David was confident King Saul wouldn't harm the priest. Priests were holy and sacred before God. He felt sure he would be safe among them. Furthermore, David knew they would welcome him, but he had no clue what he should tell Ahimelech when he arrived, especially without his men. And just as he thought, when he arrived at the town of Nob, Ahimelech, trembling, asked David, "Why are you alone? . . . Why is no one with you?" (1 Sam 21:1).

DAY 30: TUESDAY
1 SAMUEL 21:2-6

Standing before the priest, David couldn't think of any reason except the usual reason he had for visiting the priest. Still processing how to respond, he reasoned in his mind, *He doesn't know. Nobody knows that I've left—at least not yet anyway.*

Seemingly without thought, words left his mouth, "The king has sent me on a private matter" (1 Sam 21:2). David continued, "He told me not to tell anyone why I am here. I have told my men where to meet me later. Now, what is there to eat? Give me five loaves of bread or anything else you have" (1 Sam 21:2–3).

Ahimelech replied, "We don't have any regular bread. . . . But there is the holy bread, which you can have if your young men have not slept with any women recently" (1 Sam 21:4).

David then answered Ahimelech that his men were clean, that they had not been with women.

Lies, lies, lies, the thought stung his conscience. David had lied to a beloved priest of God, nonetheless. *Does Ahimelech know?* David wasn't sure. Yet, surprisingly, without a second thought, the priest gave David the consecrated bread which was unlawful for David to eat. Given his deception and state of mind, the bread tasted bland. Breaking off a piece was almost as if, symbolically, he was severing himself from his future. And with that consciousness, questions flooded his soul, *What about the promises? What about my dream of serving the king? Of being king? And my marriage to Michal—what about having a family and children?*

All his hopes seemed to flash through his mind. Each seemed to him a predestined promise that now would not happen. *I guess this is my lot in life, Lord,* David prayed. The reality of his being an outlaw and lying to the priest confirmed to him that he had no chance of any of his dreams and desires coming to pass. In a way, Saul had done what he set out to do.

I'm finished!

David chewed hard on the consecrated bread. It was dry and stale and stuck to the roof of his mouth. He had never felt as broken as he did now. He washed the bread down with a swig of wine. As he did, like Job before him, he realized what a sinful man he was. He thought of how much blood he had spilled in battle. *Is God punishing me?* His soul's answer to his own question pained him.

A man soon stole David's attention. He realized the man was Doeg, the Edomite, who cared for all of Saul's herds, and Doeg was watching him. Something about the way the shepherd looked at him made David nervous. Those shifty eyes disturbed him. And even in the solace of the house of God, David knew he was no longer safe.

DAY 31: WEDNESDAY
1 SAMUEL 21:8–9

Given the way Saul's chief herdsman was looking at him, David inquired of Ahimelech, "Don't you have a spear or a sword here? I haven't brought my sword or any other weapon, because the king's mission was urgent" (1 Sam 21:8 NIV).

The priest told David the only sword there was the one that had belonged to Goliath. Ahimelech told him, "It is wrapped in a cloth behind the ephod. If you want it, take it" (1 Sam 21:9 NIV).

"Give it here," David said.

Even as David took the sword in his hand, his mind flashed back to the first time he had seen it. There was none like it in all the world. It had belonged to the champion of a nation of giants. The sword was spectacular. He contemplated whether he would return it to the priest and figured probably not. Besides, he had lied about his reason for needing it in the first place. Now that he was officially on the run, more than likely, he would never see the priest again.

David unsheathed the sword and tested its blade. Even now, he couldn't help but remember standing over his opponent with the rock forged in Goliath's skull and that dumbfounded expression on the giant's face. *You delivered me once, and you'll deliver me again*, David thought, sheathing it.

At the same time, David couldn't help thinking to himself, *How have things turned so bad in such a short amount of time?* It seemed like just yesterday when he had been celebrated and rewarded handsomely for defeating the brute. *How has it come to this?*

Doeg the Edomite was acting skittish. David knew he was running out of time, but he needed sleep. On the way to his quarters, he made sure to flash Goliath's sword in front of the herdsman. He wouldn't do anything here and now. David was sure the king would soon know of his whereabouts. David also knew he would no longer be safe *anywhere* in Israel.

Over a good night's rest, he pondered his options and, first thing in the morning, he left Nob for the neighboring Philistine region of Gath.

DAY 32: THURSDAY
1 SAMUEL 21:10–12

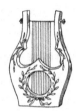

So far so good. No one has recognized me. The thought gave David some relief. He ducked his head behind his cloak as he walked through the Philistine marketplace. *Blend in. That's all you must do is blend in.* He had kept the sword of Goliath wrapped in a cloth and slung over his shoulder along with his sling. Gath was a likely place to be noticed, yet who would believe the Israelite commander who defeated their well-known champion would dare the likes of this place?

It was risky, David knew. Being in the belly of the beast would be the last place anyone would expect to find him. After Samson's eyes had been gouged out, the Philistines had underestimated Samson. They never expected he would regain his strength and push the pillars over like he had done. Of course, Samson had lost his life in the process. He had lost everything and so decided to retaliate in a last-ditch, vengeful effort. *Is that my fate?* David wondered. He certainly hoped not.

Continuing through the marketplace, he was struck by an outlandish idea, *Why not approach the king?* He had heard that Achish, the Philistine king of this area, was a reasonable man. Perhaps, David could reason with the leader and settle down in the region. He would be no threat without an army at his side.

It was another risk. He couldn't decide which was worse: making himself known or hiding in a foreign country. *What a weird place to find myself in*, David sighed. *I have a better chance of safety in the territory of the enemy than among my own kin.*

The servants of Achish were eager to lead David to their king. The way they whispered among themselves made David nervous, however. He knew his future there was up to the king, but their disdain could influence their leader to act against him.

David arrived under escort and bowed low to pay honor to the king.

"Rise," Achish insisted. "I know who you are. You're the one they sing about in their dances. What is it? 'Saul has slain his thousands, and David his tens of thousands.' Isn't that right?"

David nodded his affirmation. His mind seemed to go as fast as his heart was beating. *Was this the moment the Philistines will take me captive and gouge my eyes out as they did Samson's?*

Achish turned to his men. "Should we kill him?"

Nothing but catcalls and snide remarks followed.

Uh, oh, David gulped. But ever the warrior in battle, he began quickly sizing up his situation, and then he got an idea.

DAY 33: FRIDAY
1 SAMUEL 21:13–15

Dropping on all fours, David scurried over to one of the men standing near him and scratched at his sandal.

"Get away from me!" the guard reacted, kicking at him.

"The dogs are loud in the land of the bulls!" David snarled. He growled loudly and beat his chest. "Can you hear them?"

Everyone looked on in disbelief.

Next, David pawed at the ground with his hand and surged toward one of the servants standing by. A tray of drinks fell from the servant's hand to the ground with a *crash!* The noise didn't appear to bother David. He proceeded to knock the man to the floor. With his head lowered and his hands attached to it like horns, he began mauling the servant with them.

Some of the guards burst into laughter while others reached for their swords. David stole a glance at King Achish. For the moment, the king didn't look bothered. He appeared rather amused. *Is this actually working?* David thought as he continued to harass the servant.

Soon, he ran over and scratched at a door before howling like a wolf. He worked himself up into a frenzy. He felt foam appear on the sides of his mouth and spat wildly at the doorpost before pulling a chunk of hair from his beard; it was damp with saliva.

"I've seen enough!" the king erupted. "Look at the man! He is insane! Why bring him to me? Am I so short of madmen that you have to bring this fellow here to carry on like this in front of me? Must this man come into my house?" (1 Sam 21:14–15 NIV).

The next thing he knew, David was thrown outside on his back with a *thud!* He pounded the dusty ground before jumping up and howling again.

"Yeah, *yeah!*" a guard snickered, kicking him in the backside. "Go on! Get out of here!"

David grabbed his things and scampered away—for his life—closely watching to see if they followed him. He kept up the act until reaching the edge of the city, and then he collapsed!

"I made it!" David said under his breath. He was at the outskirts of town. He couldn't believe his acting worked. "That's one for the history books," he said to himself, and laughed. Then he laughed louder until he was no longer laughing or smiling.

Tears filled David's eyes. He had been in harm's way before and almost lost his life a number of times, but he couldn't remember a more humbling experience. The Lord had saved him before in battle. But pretending to be crazy? David sat down under a tree to rest and think. He reflected on what had just happened. He could hardly believe what he had done. He marveled that it had worked. Such an off-the-wall tactic would have never naturally come to his mind.

"It was you, God. You helped me yet again."

Humbled by the faithfulness of his God, David walked back towards the borders of Israel. He opened his mouth and out came a new song: "I will bless the Lord at all times; His praise shall continually be in my mouth. My soul shall make its boast in the Lord; the humble shall hear of it and be glad" (Ps 34:1–2 NKJV).

DAY 34: SATURDAY
REFLECTIONS FROM THE WEEK

During this week, we have seen David reach an all-time low (at least up until this point in his life) in his journey with God. Years earlier, Samuel the prophet had anointed him the next king of Israel. After saying goodbye to Jonathan and heading out of town, I can almost hear David say, "I guess the old prophet was wrong. I guess all that I thought was going to happen isn't going to happen. It must not have been meant to be. Looks like the devil won. I know I did something wrong. I messed it all up. I guess the best thing to do is gut it out. Life goes on."

I can relate, can you? Things don't work out as we thought, and then we endeavor to explain it all away.

In David's case, he leaves quietly—and alone. Maybe he thought: *It's time to start over*. Kicking some dirt on his way out of town, he began to plan, *I could always go back to shepherding*.

It reminds me of Peter after Jesus' death. There was a moment when Peter concluded: *I've missed it. I denied him, and the last three years have been for nothing.*

Even though he had seen the risen Lord, the crazy thing was, Peter went back to fishing. One day, while sitting in the boat beside his nets, Jesus showed up and gave Peter the same command He had given on the day they had first met: "Throw your net to the other side" (see John 21:6). Peter did as he was told, and another miraculous catch filled the nets. One of Peter's classic hasty responses followed. Fully clothed, he jumped overboard and swam to shore after realizing it was Jesus. Trudging toward shore, he must have thought, *Maybe there is still hope for me after all. Maybe there's still a chance I could—well, just maybe—be useful to the Master.*

After Jesus asked Peter three times if he loved Him and if he would feed His sheep, Peter was reinstated and restored to his proper place of fellowship. Not long after that, he preached to thousands and gave the very first altar call to establish the very first church. Incredible!

That was not the case with David, though. Yes, he was anointed by the same Holy Spirit that Peter was. Under the Spirit's power, David had fought lions, giants, and great battles. And where did that get him? On his way out of town with his head hung low and no evidence whatsoever he would be the next king.

Knowing he likely would never return, David ended up at Nob, a town about five miles away from Jerusalem where the priests offered sacrifices. Ahimelech was alarmed by his presence, especially by his being alone. In reading the passage, I'm guessing the priest had a good idea what was going on. Knowing how it looked, David was so desperate to inquire of the Lord that three dreadful things happened:

1. He lied about being on a mission for the king.
2. He lied again about his and his men's being consecrated and asked for provision.
3. He lied a third time about why he had no weapon.

David's three lies to the high priest remind me of Peter's three lies about knowing our Great High Priest. Then, like Peter, something remarkable happened: The unarmed David asked Ahimelech for a sword. The priest replied, "There's only one sword on the premises, and it happens to be the same sword you used to cut off Goliath's head. Go ahead and take it."

Wow! As David was slipping out the backdoor of the kingdom, it just so happened that Goliath's sword was available (and ended up in David's hands). This was no coincidence. David learned, sometimes, at our lowest point, God digs up a reminder—a holy reminder—of how faithful and good He has been before, reminding us He will be again.

I remember one low point a few years ago. I had just about given up on producing music because it seemed pointless. Unexpectedly, someone called to tell me how one of my songs brought their family member back to Christ when the individual was on his deathbed.

I believe, on a smaller scale, this was the same thing God did for David. He armed him with a weapon. And not just any weapon; it was the sword he used to overcome a huge obstacle in his life. Think about it: Every time David wielded Goliath's sword, every man he fought paled in comparison. Could it be that his Philistine opponents recognized it? There were times, in the midst of battle, David used it to intimidate his adversaries: "I used this sword to cut off Goliath's head, and you aren't half his size—or half the threat!"

What past victory has God given you? Find strength and hope in it. As David did, take the sword of past victories and wield them as weapons.

DAY 35: SUNDAY
A CLOSER LOOK AT PSALM 34

Although 116 of the Psalms have descriptions, only 73 are ascribed to David. Of those 73, only 13 give us insight to the context in which they were written during his life. Psalm 34, being one, describes the origin of the Psalm as follows: "Of David. When he pretended to be insane before Abimelek, who drove him away, and he left" (NIV) Although the wrong king is mentioned (or he was described by a different name), it is clear the Psalm refers to the event we discussed this week.

With Goliath's sword strapped on, David left the tabernacle at Nob, never to return until he was declared king. He was officially on the run, not as a deserter, but as an outlaw. At this all-time low, where was the first place David went? Gath, a region of Philistia, the land of his enemies.

There are some portions of Scriptures I read in which I think: *Did that actually happen? Is that in the Bible?* This is one of them. I find it fascinating that God used David's enemies to encourage him at one of his most difficult times.

Before Achish deemed David as a "madman," David was told by

the servants of the king: "Isn't this David, the king of the land? Isn't he the one they sing about in their dance . . . ?" (1 Sam 21:10 NIV).

The king of the land? David must have thought, *If only they knew how far that is from reality.* And yet, perhaps later, David may have been curious as to why, if his enemies could see him as king, his own people couldn't.

Here's what I think: Sometimes, our enemy's assessment of us is more accurate than that of those closest to us. Now, this is more of an observation than a truth or principle. That means it doesn't always "hold water." But let's consider why that observation can be true. It can be true because our enemy's assessment is biased against us and not for us. They have no positive inclinations or sentiments toward us.

David *had* killed tens of thousands, as opposed to Saul's thousands, and thus, in the Philistines' minds, he *must* be king. But here's the danger of trying to side with, find comfort in, or settle down (live with) your enemy: Although they correctly pegged David, they also wanted to kill him. *Yikes!* And that's worth remembering.

There's only one statement I can think of that fits David's response: "And the Oscar goes to—David, future King of Israel." His acting was incredible, or should I say, the fact that his enemies believed he was crazy was amazing!

In all the research I have done on David's life journey, I can't think of a more humbling experience. As he left (or was driven away) by King Achish, the first line in the Psalm of praise he sang was, "I will bless the Lord at all times." Let's look more closely at Psalm 34:1 in a few translations:

> I will bless the Lord at all times: His praise shall continually be in my mouth (KJV).

I will extol the Lord at all times; His praise will always be on my lips (NIV).

I will praise the Lord no matter what happens. I will constantly speak of His glories and grace (TLB).

I bless God every chance I get; my lungs expand with His praise (MSG).

Thousands of songs have been penned based on this one Psalm. Of these, some will be sung for thousands or millions of years (in eternity). If God exalts the humble (see James 4:10), then look how God has used just the opening line of this Psalm, written in David's most humble of times, to inspire the world.

If you find yourself at an all-time low (tragic, horrific, or otherwise), read Psalm 34 and allow it to fill your sails with hope and fuel your desire to continually bless and praise God:

I will bless the Lord at all times; His praise shall continually be in my mouth. My soul shall make its boast in the Lord; the humble shall hear of it and be glad. Oh, magnify the Lord with me, and let us exalt His name together. I sought the Lord, and He heard me, and delivered me from all my fears. They looked to Him and were radiant, and their faces were not ashamed. This poor man cried out, and the Lord heard him, and saved him out of all his troubles. The angel of the Lord encamps all around those who fear Him, and delivers them. Oh, taste and see that the Lord is good; blessed is the man who trusts in Him! Oh, fear the Lord, you His saints! There is no want to those who fear Him. The young lions lack and suffer hunger; but those who seek the Lord shall not lack any good thing (Ps 34:1–10 NKJV).

WEEK 6
CAVE EXPERIENCES

DAY 36: MONDAY
1 SAMUEL 22:1

After David left Gath, he could think of only one place to go. It was on the outskirts of Israel, in Judah. During military campaigns, he and his men had camped there a few times. More than anything, what he liked about the region or stronghold, as it was called, were the caves surrounding it—in particular, the cave of Adullam.

Even on his way there, he knew people would recognize him. There was no point in his trying to disguise himself. To children and their parents alike, David was, and would always be, the giant-slayer! Uncloaking Goliath's sword, he strapped it to his side. Should he have to use it, it would be easier to access there.

David arrived alone and built a fire. He knew it was going to be a rough night. He looked around at the cave walls and felt them closing in around him. All at once, he blurted, "Where *do* I belong, God? I don't seem to be welcomed in Israel or Judah. And I can't go home!" David poked at the fire with a stick. "I can't even find safety in a foreign land!" David had never felt too trapped—or helpless. There, separated from his mother, father, brothers, wife, men, and

Jonathan, he couldn't help but feel angry. As he jabbed at the sparking tinder, one agonizing thought burned through his emotional state: *You are alone, David, all alone.*

David chucked the stick in his hand. With a loud *thump*, it smashed against the wall, echoing loudly throughout the cavern. He felt silly, embarrassed for his outburst—his tantrum. Hopelessness tried to grasp him around the neck and pull him under. He physically struggled for breath. He fought it, and instead of letting his anger turn to rage (as was Saul's way of dealing with such things), he exhaled and prayed:

When I am overwhelmed, you alone know the way I should turn. Wherever I go, my enemies have set traps for me. I look for someone to come and help me, but no one gives me a passing thought! No one will help me; no one cares a bit what happens to me. Then I pray to you, O Lord. I say, "You are my place of refuge. You are all I really want in life. Hear my cry, for I am very low" (Ps 142:3–7).

David paused. "I *am* alive," he said. "And for that I'm grateful." After looking at his surroundings, David whispered, "Some help and companionship would sure be nice."

DAY 37: TUESDAY
1 SAMUEL 22:2

After a few hours of light sleep, David awoke with a gasp. *Where am I?* He couldn't place the beads of sunlight shining on the cavern walls. The fire had fizzled out and smoldered slightly. Only then did he remember where he was. David forced himself to his feet, yawned, and stretched, feeling a tightness wring his spine. Cave floors were unbearably hard.

It had been almost dark when he arrived the night before. Now, outside in the light of sunrise, he could see everything. It was more brilliant than he remembered, and yet, as he peered out over the Valley of Elah, David felt a tinge of sadness. On the open plain was where he had killed Goliath. In a single moment, everything had changed with the giant's defeat. He couldn't quite see where it had happened, though. But he didn't need to see the exact spot to remember—vividly—how God had given him victory that day.

The sight of a distant rider suddenly snapped David out of his daydream. He watched carefully to see if the man was alone. He was. David took his eyes away only long enough to grab his sword. *Friend or foe?* he wondered.

Simply because the man waved to him didn't mean the man could be trusted. *Surely this soon, Saul couldn't have found out about my whereabouts. No, this man can't be from Saul. A spy, maybe, but not an assassin.* The closer the rider came, the more David saw how massive he was. The man was no Goliath by any means, but David held tight to his sword, nonetheless.

"Who are you, and where do you come from?" David yelled to him as the rider slowed to a trot.

"My name is Benaiah son of Jehoiada," the man replied. "And I mean you no harm. You are David. Isn't that right?"

"That's close enough," David commanded and waited until the rider slowed to a stop. "What do you want with David?"

"I'm from Kabzeel, originally. But I heard from a man in the region of Gath that David came this way."

"Yes, I was. And, let me explain," Benaiah said, dismounting his horse. "Your servant was in Gath for fear of his life. I was—well—let's just say I'm not welcome there anymore because of a disagreement with one of my neighbors who was found dead."

David watched and listened intently, never taking his hand from his sword.

"Although I wanted to," Benaiah explained, "I didn't kill him though I had the opportunity to many times. And, to be honest with you, after all he had done, it's what he deserved. I pleaded my case, but no one believed me. As you can see—"

"No need to explain. I know what it is to be falsely accused," David interrupted. "But you didn't answer my question. What do you want with David?"

"I've heard about David's conquests. And his victories," Benaiah replied, walking towards him. David walked out to meet him. "And, since I'm an outlaw now. Well, I don't know. When I heard he was in the region, I wondered if he might be willing to help me."

"You are in good company, my friend," David said, shaking his hand. "Your servant, David, is also an outlaw, wrongly accused by many in Israel, including the king."

Benaiah didn't reply, but his face told the story.

"And, although I am looked upon with disfavor by those whom I previously served, my answer is, yes. I will surely help you."

"Thank you," Benaiah said. "I pledge myself to serve you—with my life."

"And I you," David replied.

As they retreated into the cave, David couldn't help but think of his prayer. God had heard his cry for help. And before the day was over, two others arrived: Shammah son of Agee from Harar and Eleazar son of Dodai, a descendant of Ahoah.

"Then others began coming—men who were in trouble or in debt or who were just discontented—until David was the captain of about 400 men" (1 Sam. 22:2). And from that day on, he was never alone.

DAY 38: WEDNESDAY
1 SAMUEL 22:1–4, 11–23; 2 SAMUEL 23:15–17

Night after night, around the glow of campfire, David and his men got acquainted. The men came to respect his wisdom as a leader, a man of war, and a man of God. The strength of this brotherhood grew so strong that he and his men were inseparable.

One night, David mentioned in passing, "Oh, how I would love some of that good water from the well by the gate in Bethlehem."

Without his knowing, three of his men who overheard his request broke through the Philistine lines, drew some water from the well by the gate in Bethlehem, and brought it back to him. David looked down at the cup of water in his hand and, to their horror, refused to drink it. Instead, he poured it out as a drink offering to the Lord. They didn't seem all that surprised—disgusted maybe, but not surprised. Many of the things David did appeared strange to them.

"God forbid I should drink this!" he shouted. "This water is as precious as the blood of these men who risked their lives to bring it to me" (2 Sam. 23:17).

"Figures," he heard someone say. *Sounded like Benaiah*, he thought to himself. Although he was grateful, David didn't care much about their response.

The next morning, a man approached their camp who David recognized—barely—because he looked so haggard. It was Abiathar, one of the priests of Nob.

"What did King Saul do?" David asked Abiathar. "Speak clearly, and slow down!"

"I'm telling you! The king has gone mad! He was so angry with you when you came and saw my father that he killed them."

"He killed your father?" David asked, shocked.

"No! Not only my father, he killed all eighty of the priests at Nob—my entire household! And I was the only one who escaped to come tell you."

David roared, "I knew it! When I saw Doeg the Edomite there that day, I knew he was sure to tell Saul. Now I have caused the death of all your father's family. Stay here with me, and don't be afraid. I will protect you with my own life, for the same person wants to kill us both" (1 Sam 22:22–23).

"Thank you," Abiathar replied. "I'm tired, and I'd like to rest now."

"Yes, of course." David commanded one of his men, "Make a place for the priest in my tent. He has had a very sorrowful journey."

Benaiah, Shammah, and Eleazar followed David as he walked away. He looked to the ground and muttered, "Is there no end to his rage?" The three said nothing as they walked with him.

More men arrived later that day. David was always pleased when others came. And yet, one thought lingered—one thought David couldn't shake: *Saul will stop at nothing until he has found and killed me.* And David realized his family would never be safe.

"I need you to do something for me," he told his three captains.

"Anything," Shammah said.

"Take some men and go get my parents from Bethlehem. Bring them here because they are no longer safe."

A few days later, to David's relief, his entire family—his father, mother, and brothers—arrived safely. To his surprise, his brothers didn't hesitate to join his rag-tag army of misfits. Afterward, David went to Mizpeh in Moab and asked the king, "Please allow my father and mother to live here with you until I know what God is going to do for me" (1 Sam 22:3). The king permitted them to stay with him the entire time David was in the stronghold.

David's parents stayed in Moab with the king during the entire time David was living in his stronghold.

DAY 39: THURSDAY
1 SAMUEL 22:5; 23:1–29

David and his men camped near the cave of Adullam until being warned by the prophet, Gad, that they were no longer safe there. David turned toward Judah and hid in the forest of Hereth.

As difficult as it was to believe what Saul had done to the priests at Nob, David was grateful for one thing: Abiathar, Ahimelech's son. On a continual basis, the young priest inquired of the Lord for David.

One such occasion was over the Philistine conquest of Keilah, a nearby Jewish city. After saving the city, David learned Saul and his army were coming to Keilah. Via Abiathar, David inquired of the Lord who answered, "If you stay here, this city will betray you and hand you over to King Saul." Upon hearing this, David and approximately six hundred men moved from Keilah into the countryside. "Word soon reached Saul that David had escaped, so he didn't go to Keilah after all. David now stayed in the strongholds of the wilderness and in the hill country of Ziph. Saul hunted him day after day, but God didn't let Saul find him" (1 Sam 23:13–14).

While in the wilderness, Jonathan snuck away and privately met with David. David embraced his friend with joy. "How did you get free to come see me? You risk too much!"

"It was dangerous, but I had to come," Jonathan replied. "I'm done, though. I cannot support my father any longer in this crazy escapade to find and kill you."

"Thank you," David said. "I still don't know what I did to—"

Jonathan assured him, "Don't be afraid ... My father will never find you! You are going to be the king of Israel, and I will be next to you, as my father, Saul, is well aware" (1 Sam 23:17).

After renewing their covenant before the Lord, David remained in Horesh, and Jonathan went back home.

King? David wondered. *Is Jonathan as crazy as his father? How will I ever be king, especially now?*

Even while Jonathan met with his friend, the men of Ziph betrayed David and tried to hand him over to Saul. It was a close call, but Jonathan was right—Saul could never pin David down.

At one point, the two were on the same mountain, and Saul's men were closing in on David when they received a message of a Philistine raid on Israel. Saul and his men left their pursuit of David to return home to fight the Philistines. The place where David was camped when this happened became known as "the Rock of Escape. David then went to live in the strongholds of En-gedi" (1 Sam 23:28–29).

After this close call, David sang to the Lord, "I cry out to the Lord; I plead for the Lord's mercy. I pour out my complaints before him and tell him all my troubles. When I am overwhelmed, you alone know the way I should turn" (Ps 142:1–3).

DAY 40: FRIDAY
1 SAMUEL 24

After returning from his fight with the Philistines, Saul was informed of David's location. From Israel, he chose three thousand elite troops to hunt down David. Near the rocks of the wild goats in the wilderness of En-gedi, Saul left his men and retreated into a cave to relieve himself. David and his men happened to be hiding further back in the very same cave.

His men nudged him. "Isn't that the king?"

David couldn't believe his eyes.

"Now's your opportunity!" David's men whispered to him. "Today the Lord is telling you, 'I will certainly put your enemy into your power, to do with as you wish'" (1 Sam 24:4). So David crept up to the king and cut off a piece of the hem of the king's robe.

In his trembling hand, David clutched the fabric he had cut from Saul's robe. Something didn't feel right. His heart hurt, and his stomach was in knots. *I could have killed him*, David reminded himself. *Maybe I should have killed him.* And yet everything felt wrong. He wondered if his emotions were betraying him. Perhaps, he was afraid, or was it something else?

David had killed many men—many Philistines, including Goliath. *But a fellow Israelite—the king, nonetheless?* And that's when David knew something his men would not understand. Before God Almighty, he absolutely *knew* he must not harm the king. Why? Because King Saul was *God's anointed*.

David was mortified when he learned Saul killed the priests at Nob. And there in the cave, he realized: *Saul killed them to achieve his own desire of getting to me*. And more than that, David acknowledged, *If I killed Saul to attain the crown, I would be no different*. Saul had always done what was in his own best interest, as well as what made himself look good in front of the people.

Although his men would not like it, David had a choice to make. And upon returning, he said to them, "The Lord forbid that I should do this to my lord the king. I shouldn't attack the Lord's anointed one, for the Lord Himself has chosen him" (1 Sam 24:6). David then kept his men from killing Saul.

It was a hard call, and even though his men doubted the logic at first, David felt peace concerning his decision. After following Saul outside the cave and getting his attention, David held up the piece of cloth he had cut away. Saul looked down, ashamed, when he noticed the piece missing from his robe.

David bowed low and yelled, "May the Lord judge between us. Perhaps the Lord will punish you for what you are trying to do to me, but I will never harm you. . . . May the Lord therefore judge which of us is right and punish the guilty one. He is my advocate, and He will rescue me from your power!" (1 Sam 24:12, 15).

Saul wept bitterly when he realized what David had done. David closely watched his men. They were very much interested in what the king would say next, and David couldn't have been more pleased with Saul's response as the king recognized David's kindness in not killing him. Saul said, "May the Lord reward you well for the kindness you have shown me today. And now I realize that you are surely going to be king, and that the kingdom of Israel will flourish under your rule. Now swear to me by the Lord that when that happens you will not kill my family and destroy my line of descendants!" (1 Sam 24:19–21).

In the presence of his men, David agreed with the king's request, promising to do Saul's descendants no harm. With that, Saul returned to his home, David and his men to Adullam.

On the way back to the stronghold, Benaiah, Shammah, and Eleazar rode up next to their commander. "In God's eyes, there's a right way to be promoted to power," David explained. "Even with all the wrong he's done and his long list of shortcomings, killing Saul, God's anointed, is not the right thing to do—ever."

"We get it now," they said. "And the men do as well."

DAY 41: SATURDAY
REFLECTIONS FROM THE WEEK

What was the most defining moment in David's life? Was it during a profound encounter of worship in the shepherd's pasture? Was it when Samuel anointed him the next king of Israel? Was it the moment he defeated Goliath the Philistine? Or was it when he became king?

All these are great instances in David's journey, and I've certainly gleaned from them. But in my opinion, they pale in comparison to the days David spent hiding and dodging death as an outlaw on the run from Saul. And of those times where, by and large, David wrote some of his most astounding worship material, a single defining moment stands out in my mind above the rest. Here is how the Scripture recounts it, "A cave was there, and Saul went in to relieve himself. David and his men were far back in the cave" (1 Sam 24:3 NIV).

Finally, David caught a break. His men were thrilled and were quick to offer advice such as: "The Lord be praised! It's over, David. God has heard your prayers and handed your enemy over to you." It sounded correct. It sounded logical. And I'm sure David took a step back and thought: *Yeah, that sounds right. Of all the caves the king could have wandered into, he enters this one—and all alone. Now's my chance to kill him.* And for a split second, I'm sure David was tempted to believe this deception. And who wouldn't? It made perfect sense.

Slyly, David crept up to where Saul was relieving himself and cut off a section of Saul's kingly garment. The only problem with this act was: Years earlier, Samuel had prophesied about this very garment. It was no ordinary robe. It was the king's garment in which Samuel had declared (speaking of Saul and David): "The Lord has *torn* the kingdom of Israel from you [Saul] today and has *given* it to your neighbor [David], who is better than you" (1 Sam 15:28 NASB, emphasis mine).

Why was the prophecy significant? This encounter with the king was undeniably orchestrated by God, but not for David's deliverance. Rather, David was being tested, but not as much for the testing as to teach him an important lesson: A kingly garment being *torn* and *given* by God is much different than a kingly garment being *cut* and *taken* by man.

When David cut the king's garment, he was defiling his future position. Symbolically, he cut the clothes he would someday be wearing. That's why he felt ashamed afterward. And this lesson is what many today don't understand about honoring leadership, even those leaders who are acting inappropriately. How David honored Saul (even as unjustly as he was being treated) determined how he would someday be given honor.

Some might think: *Wait a minute? Wasn't the king overthrown by his own son, Absalom?* Yes, he was. But Absalom's early death confirms my point. Absalom's reign was destined for destruction at its inception from failure to learn this very lesson. Absalom cut the kingdom out from under his father, David. It was not *given to* him but rather *taken by* him, which led to his demise.

Unlike Absalom, years earlier, after cutting Saul's garment, Scripture states that David was: "Conscience-stricken for having cut off a corner of" the king's robe (1 Sam 24:5 NIV).

David's men didn't understand; how could they? They were not *men* after God's own heart, nor were they accountable for David's actions. David alone, a *man* after God's own heart, was responsible for the treatment of the royal kingly garment.

It's also interesting that David was not tested in a royal palace but rather in a slimy outhouse. And there in a smelly cave, before a crown was ever placed on his head—before he took a scepter in his hand or sat on a golden throne—in the sight of God and his men, David was tested. This defining moment not only secured David's future, but it also allowed God to establish His Kingdom forever.

DAY 42: SUNDAY
A CLOSER LOOK AT PSALM 142

It seems that our culture today has elevated the "Steady Eddies" who know how to temper down their emotions and maintain consistency. These level-headed thinkers are celebrated. Even in the church, the moment people start getting too crazy, they're looked down upon. People say things like: "It's just hype—mere sensationalism, all emotionalism, Holy Spirit mumbo jumbo."

I'm confident, had David been evaluated by a psychologist today, he would have been diagnosed as bipolar or clinically depressed. In one breath, David sang songs like, "I can't go on because God is nowhere in sight and has given victory over to the wicked. We're all going to die!" In the next stanza of the same song, he would sing, "But there's no need to worry. It'll be okay. Put your hope in God because He's going to save us."

David also did irrational things that made everyone around him scratch their heads in bewilderment. After mentioning he wanted some water from the well of Bethlehem, his men risked their lives to get him a single cup. And what did David do? He poured it out as a drink offering. Who does that? And weren't drink offerings supposed to be made with wine? Was he making this stuff up as he went?

This *is* the only time in the Old Testament we see a drink offering of water. I wonder if David (the line from which Jesus, the Messiah, came) was forecasting that, not only blood would be poured out on the cross, but water from the Lord's side. Later, the disciple whom the Lord loved recalled Jesus being born of both water and blood (1 John 5:6).

Like Jesus' time on the cross, David's time in the cave of Adullam was one of his loneliest times. It almost sounds like a nervous breakdown when he loses it before God and prays: "I cry out to the Lord; I plead for the Lord's mercy. I *pour out* my complaints before Him and tell Him all my troubles" (Ps 142:1–2, emphasis mine).

I like to compare Psalm 142 to Elijah's rant after calling down fire from heaven. I believe his tirade is the equivalent to David's Psalm. Soon after debasing and killing the prophets of Baal, while running for his life, Elijah found himself discouraged and alone. He said: "I have zealously served the Lord God Almighty. But the people of Israel have broken their covenant with You, torn down Your altars, and killed every one of Your prophets. I am the only one left, and now they are trying to kill me, too" (1 Kgs 19:14).

That sounds familiar to David's outburst in Psalm 142:4, where he said, "I look for someone to come and help me, but no one gives me a passing thought! No one will help me; no one cares a bit what happens to me."

In both David's and Elijah's moments of despair, their chief complaint was: "I'm tired, alone, and I don't see an answer in sight. Come on, God. A little help would be nice!"

God was quick to remind Elijah that he was *not* the only prophet left. In fact, there was a remnant of seven thousand who had not bowed their knees and worshiped Baal. And in David's case, God began to send warriors to him—four hundred at first, and eventually a battalion of six hundred. The only problem with those God sent David was they were disgruntled, in distress, outlaws, in debt, and discontented. I'm sure David looked at God's answer and must have thought: *These people are my help? This group? Really, God?*

I tend to agree with David. Why would God surround David with the underdogs of the kingdom given David's battle for his life?

The last few verses of Psalm 142 give us a glimpse as to the reason: "Hear my cry, for I am very low. Rescue me from my persecutors, for they are too strong for me. Bring me out of prison so I can thank You. The godly will crowd around me, for You are good to me" (vv 6–7).

At the time of their arrival, I'd say the crowd around David was anything but *godly*. Near the end of his life, some decades later, David described his most loyal servants and mightiest of warriors—who did great exploits and helped establish the kingdom—as those who pursued and followed him during his difficult time in the cave (read 2 Sam 23:8–39). David's mighty men (as they were called) were once underdogs who proved their diligence and worth before—not after—David became king.

Have you cried out to God for answers? Have you asked God for help? Perhaps, the people God sent your way are a little rough around the edges. Perhaps, they are underdogs. They may even be in debt, disgruntled, and downright discouraged. Watch out, because, as David found out, they could become your greatest friends and allies.

WEEK 7
NEW WIVES

DAY 43: MONDAY
1 SAMUEL 25:1–2

In David's last encounter with Saul, where he spared the king's life, David held onto Saul's promise not to pursue him any longer. A few years later, Saul had kept that promise. Meanwhile, David enjoyed some peace, if you want to call being a wanderer *peaceful*.

In those years, David lost and gained men. Their loyalty was proven through time. Those who believed he would quickly rise to power eventually left. Those whose commitment was unwavering stayed. In the course of time, one such warrior became a great asset to David's ranks: Abishai son of Zeruiah, David's nephew. His younger brother Asahel accompanied Abishai when they approached David's camp. David looked for their other brother, Joab, a brilliant military mind and brave warrior, but didn't see him.

David rode out to meet them. "Greetings. How goes the war and Israel's campaigns against the Lord's enemies?"

"Not well," Abishai replied.

David was taken aback by his nephew's candor.

"And your brother Joab? How is he?"

"Our brother is well and taking care of our family's needs," Asahel answered. "He's not coming."

"I see." David was disappointed. He could use a great military strategist like his nephew, Joab. "Well, I'm glad you've come."

"With the current state of Israel and Saul's misfortune on the battlefield, we wish to join your ranks—if you'll have us?" Abishai said.

David turned to his men. They gave no reply and didn't need to; their faces told the story. More people were more mouths to feed. More importantly, more family meant more awkwardness among the ranks.

David noticed those jockeying for position seemed a bit squeamish—seeming to object. Before any controversy arose, David made his decision. "You will have the opportunity—just as those you see— to prove your loyalty. No one is forcing anyone to come, or stay. All I ask is that, when you're here—you're fully here."

"Of course," Asahel agreed.

"But there is another matter at hand," Abishai said. "I'm afraid I come bearing bad news."

More bad news about the king? Has he been hurt? Oh no, was it Jonathan? David braced himself for the news.

"I'm sorry to say, Israel's beloved prophet, Samuel, is dead. All Israel has gathered to bury him near his house in Ramah. I know you would have liked to have been there to pay your respects. But we both know that probably wouldn't be a good idea."

David's men agreed.

The news shook David to the core. Samuel had started this whole crazy journey. David thought back to the day he met the prophet. *What was I, just fifteen*, he reminisced. Samuel had anointed him the next king. *Has the prophecy died with the prophet?* David couldn't help but wonder.

David and his men, along with their new additions, Abishai and Asahel, mourned for Samuel many days before moving to a new location down in the wilderness of Maon.

DAY 44: TUESDAY
1 SAMUEL 25:4–31

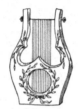

David felt right at home in Maon. It was sheep country and reminded him of his upbringing. For more than a year, he camped in the region and provided protection for several flocks. Once the Midianites found out David and his small army camped there, they didn't dare threaten the pastureland. After doing some research, David discovered the flocks belonged to a man named Nabal, a descendant of Caleb, who lived in Carmel.

Around sheep shearing season, when David's provisions were running low, he sent a few young men (about ten) from his ranks with a message to Nabal, asking him for some food. Nabal's reply was less than hospitable:

> Who does this son of Jesse think he is? There are lots of servants these days who run away from their masters. Should I take my bread and my water and my meat that I've slaughtered for my shearers and give it to a band of outlaws who come from who knows where? (1 Sam 25:10–11).

When the men returned and told David what Nabal had said, David was furious and rallied four hundred of his men to attack Nabal's household. As they were on their way to do so, a small caravan met them. It was led by a woman named Abigail, Nabal's wife. She quickly dismounted her donkey and bowed before David, saying, "I accept all blame in this matter, my lord. Please listen to what I have to say. I know Nabal is a wicked and ill-tempered man; please don't pay any attention to him. He is a fool, just as his name suggests. But I never even saw the young men you sent" (1 Sam 25:23–25).

David noticed how beautiful Abigail was, and how she carried herself with rare poise and dignity. Not only that, but she came bearing gifts—two hundred loaves of bread, two wineskins full of wine, five sheep that had been slaughtered, nearly a bushel of roasted grain, one hundred clusters of raisins, and two hundred fig cakes.

Abigail not only thanked David and his men, she also encouraged them and complimented them for protecting their flocks. It had been a frivolous season where David felt nothing important was happening regarding his future destiny, so Abigail's words caught him off guard, when she said,

> The Lord will surely reward you with a lasting dynasty, for you are fighting the Lord's battles. And you have not done wrong throughout your entire life. . . . When the Lord has done all He promised and has made you leader of Israel, don't let this be a blemish on your record. Then your conscience won't have to bear the staggering burden of needless bloodshed and vengeance (1 Sam 25:28, 30–31).

David was impressed. How did this young—and beautiful—woman have such wisdom and knowledge? She also seemed to understand a great deal about his life and all he had been through and, more importantly, where he was going. He considered her words, *Is she right? Will I regret my actions if I answer this fool according to his folly? How did such a scoundrel end up with such a dignified and diplomatic wife?*

David couldn't help what popped into his mind next, *I wouldn't mind having a wife like her, should the opportunity ever present itself.* David scolded himself for thinking such a covetous thought and disregarded it. *That'll never happen,* he assumed.

DAY 45: WEDNESDAY
1 SAMUEL 25:31–42

David snapped out of his fantasy world as Abigail finished her speech. Her final words waxed elegant: "And when the Lord has done these great things for you, please remember me, your servant!" (1 Sam 25:31).

David cleared his throat and looked over to his men, who also seemed to be enjoying the woman's discourse. He waxed grateful in return, if not stately, as he said to her, "Praise the Lord, the God of Israel, who has sent you to meet me today! Thank God for your good sense! Bless you for keeping me from murder and from carrying out vengeance with my own hands. For I swear by the Lord, the God of Israel, who has kept me from hurting you, that if you had not hurried out to meet me, not one of Nabal's men would still be alive tomorrow morning" (1 Sam 25:32–34).

Having said that, David accepted her gifts and then assured her that she could go home and he would not kill her husband.

Abishai rode up next to David on their way back to camp, "Well, was that interesting, or what?"

"Yes, it was," David replied.

"Hearing such a woman as that surely causes you to miss your wife, Michal, the king's daughter?"

"It does."

All the way back to camp, Abigail's words resonated through David's mind: *Please remember me, your servant.* David chuckled to himself. *How can I forget her?*

All week, David thanked God again for sparing him from the shedding of blood. As shrewd as Nabal was, David couldn't believe the nerve of the man. *I was about to kill his entire household.* The thought embarrassed him and made him feel small.

Ten days later, David received some very surprising news. "Nabal is dead," a servant told him. "The Lord struck him down, and he died in his sleep."

David couldn't help but think of the words of Moses about vengeance belonging to God alone—that He will repay.

After learning the news, David sat down with his harp and sang these words: "O Lord, the God of vengeance, O God of vengeance, let Your glorious justice shine forth! Arise, O Judge of the earth. Give the proud what they deserve" (Ps 94:1–2).

David learned a valuable lesson from the experience: *I don't need to defend myself. God will do that for me.* It was a lesson that applied to the wicked Nabal, and it also gave him hope for what Saul had taken from him, including his wife, Michal. After the entire ordeal, one thought remained: *What will happen to Nabal's wife, Abigail?* David thought long and hard on that one.

Soon, he sent messengers to her, asking her to become his wife. When the servants arrived and told her that they were to take her to David—to marry him—she said, "I, your servant, would be happy to marry David" (1 Sam 25:42). Taking her attendants with her, she went and became David's wife.

DAY 46: THURSDAY
1 SAMUEL 25:43–44; 26:1–17

Things were changing for David. Yes, he was an outlaw. But for how long? For a while, he believed God might remove the wicked Saul. As time kept dragging on, however, he gave up on the idea. One thing he knew for sure: It was out of his hands. Rolling up his sleeves, David settled in for the long haul, not for a few months or years or even decades. To make matters worse, David heard his wife, Michal, had been given to another man.

He's just trying to get under my skin, David stewed. Upon receiving the news, he didn't feel so bad about marrying Abigail. In fact, he also decided to take another wife, Ahinoam from Jezreel. He couldn't live in limbo for a decade. He had to move on with his life.

One day, more bad news arrived. After a few years of peace, David learned Saul had gathered three thousand of Israel's finest warriors to hunt him once again. *Will this never end?* He sighed.

When Saul and his army reached Hakilah, just a few short miles away from where David and his men were hiding, he sent spies to the camp. Once their location was confirmed, David and Abishai snuck down near the camp at night. It was quiet, chillingly quiet.

Abishai didn't hold back but walked right down into the camp without hesitation.

"What are you doing?" David whispered.

For whatever reason, and contrary to sound judgment, David was compelled to follow. As the two men walked in and throughout the tents, no one stirred. Even the crickets were silent. *This is weird!*

It didn't take long to find Saul's tent, the kingly spear stuck firmly in the ground outside. David stopped and looked long and hard at the king's spear before turning to Abishai. They both glanced around the camp and suddenly realized the whole camp had been lulled to sleep by the power of God. *But why? What was God up to?* David wanted to know.

Just about that time, Abishai grabbed his arm and pulled him closer to Saul's tent, whispering to him, "God has surely handed your enemy over to you this time! . . . Let me pin him to the ground with one thrust of the spear; I won't need to strike twice!" (1 Sam 26:8).

David pulled away. *I've already had the opportunity to take Saul's life once*, he remembered. *And here I am with Abishai, one of the few not there with me on that day.* It was a perfect storm, David knew. The deep sleep coming upon the entire camp and having Abishai by his side were not coincidence. And, because David realized God was testing him for the second time, he responded,

> Don't kill him. For who can remain innocent after attacking the Lord's anointed one? Surely the Lord will strike Saul down someday, or he will die of old age or in battle. The Lord forbid that I should kill the one He has anointed! But take his spear and that jug of water beside his head, and then let's get out of here! (1 Sam 26:9–11).

The two men left and then climbed the hill opposite the camp until they were a safe distance away. David turned back and yelled to

Saul's chief commander, Abner, "Where in all Israel is there anyone as mighty? So why haven't you guarded your master the king when someone came to kill him? This isn't good at all! I swear by the Lord that you and your men deserve to die, because you failed to protect your master, the Lord's anointed! Look around! Where are the king's spear and the jug of water that were beside his head?" (1 Sam 26:15–16).

"Is that you, my son?" The voice that answered caused a chill to work its way down David's spine. It was not the voice of Abner, but after years of no contact, David heard the voice of his father-in-law; it was that of King Saul.

DAY 47: FRIDAY
1 SAMUEL 26:17–27:4

Just the sound of the king's voice brought back all the questions David had asked himself through the years. This was his opportunity to seek an answer from the very one who had set him to flight.

"Yes, my lord the king. Why are you chasing me? What have I done? What is my crime? . . . Why has the king of Israel come out to search for a single flea? Why does he hunt me down like a partridge on the mountains?" (1 Sam 26:17–20).

Then came Saul's confession, "I have sinned. Come back home, my son, and I will no longer try to harm you, for you valued my life today. I have been a fool and very, very wrong" (1 Sam 26:17, 20–21).

David remembered cutting a piece off the king's robe. He was not about to make the same mistake twice. Thus, he instructed one of Saul's servants to retrieve the items he had stolen. They belonged to the king, and to the king they would return.

As quickly as the encounter had occurred, it was over. Saul blessed David, and they parted ways.

On David's way back with Abishai, neither spoke to the other for some time. David was sure he knew the reason but broke the silence and asked anyway, "What's wrong?"

"I just don't understand why, when the Lord handed your enemy over to you, you would do nothing? I mean, come on, you saw what God did to the camp by placing them in a deep slumber? Surely, God did that for a reason?"

"Yes, I know," David replied.

What was the reason? David wondered. *Was it only to test me yet again?* Saul's life was his for the taking. Had he been right to turn it down?

"You're going to have to trust me," David told his nephew.

"You know I trust you," Abishai said.

Do I trust my decision? David couldn't help thinking. Because he chose to leave the king unharmed, David had once again avoided death. But for how long this time? *How long before Saul comes after me again?* His mind struggled with the constant threat of Saul's pursuit. And then David had a very strange thought: *There's a difference between praying for God to save me time after time and putting myself in harm's way.* It appeared that, as long as Saul was alive, David understood he would never be safe in Israel. And if he continued to stay where he was, then his life would be in jeopardy.

David kept thinking, "Someday Saul is going to get me. The best thing I can do is escape to the Philistines. Then Saul will stop hunting for me in Israelite territory, and I will finally be safe" (1 Sam 27:1).

"Are you sure you trust me?" David asked Abishai.

"You know I do," Abishai replied. "No matter what."

"Good," David said. "Because I think it's time we leave Israel, before Saul succeeds in finding and killing me. It's just a matter of time."

"My brother and I, as well as the men, are with you."

David took Abishai and his six hundred men and joined Achish son of Maoch, the king of Gath. His two wives went with them.

When Saul heard that David fled to Gath, he discontinued his pursuit of his son-in-law.

DAY 48: SATURDAY
REFLECTIONS FROM THE WEEK

I've had two very difficult seasons in which, financially, we needed a massive breakthrough. In both cases, around the time of each financial obstacle, a tempting opportunity presented itself. Both opportunities, however, came with strings attached, causing me to hesitate in accepting the offers. At the same time, both opportunities appeared to be a shortcut to success.

During this week's readings, David experienced a second tempting opportunity to fast track his ascension to the throne of Israel. In both cases, it was as if God gift-wrapped David's enemy—once in the cave and once in Saul's camp. In the cave, David was encouraged by his men to take Saul's life, and in the camp, his trusted nephew, Abishai, encouraged him to take what was rightfully his.

At the point when the deadline was approaching and our financial picture looked rather bleak, I remember turning to my wife and asking her, "How is your faith right now? Do you feel your faith is strong enough to make God our *only* option?"

She thought for a minute, and with confidence in her eyes

replied, "My faith is strong. If you feel good, I'm okay with turning down the money and making God our only option."

After we both agreed and resolved in our hearts to refuse the tempting offer, we prayed together and placed our trust in God to provide. The next day, a young couple who had been attending our church, met with us and said, "God spoke to us last night, and we wanted to give you something." They went on to hand us a check for twenty thousand dollars, which was more than we needed.

I rejoiced and thanked God, but in the back of my mind, I wondered why God would test us twice—both in the very same way. While contemplating this, I felt God lead me to the story of Joseph. In one day, Joseph was brought from the prison to the palace to interpret Pharaoh's two dreams. You notice Pharaoh had *two* dreams (not one), concerning the coming seven years of famine. Joseph told Pharaoh: "The reason the dream was given to Pharaoh in two forms is that the matter has been firmly decided by God, and God will do it soon" (Gen 41:32 NIV).

When I think about the two tests that came our way—both offering me the easy way out—it reminds me of the two tests David encountered. In each case, David was handed the king's life. He could have easily taken the crown for himself—by force—but instead, he decided not to lay a hand on Saul, allowing God to work on his behalf. What did David do besides successfully pass each test? David made God his *only* option!

I believe, because he did so, he passed both tests. And because he passed both tests (both orchestrated by God), as with Pharaoh's dream about the famine, David's ascent to the throne was "firmly decided by God"!

David was saying, "When, or if, I ever become king of Israel, it's going to be because God did it." As with his intent to destroy Nabal, had David taken matters into his own hands, he would have shed much blood and lost out on having the noble woman, Abigail, as a wife. David was patient at letting God fulfill His plan and reaped the rewards.

Are you trying to help God out? I wonder if those tempting opportunities that make achieving breakthrough easier (without going the distance) are a test from God? David had that opportunity to take what was rightfully his, but he decided not to take matters into own hands. Instead, he trusted God to make it happen. Maybe, as David did, and as I experienced, God wants you to make Him your *only* option!

DAY 49: SUNDAY
A CLOSER LOOK AT PSALM 54

Psalm 54 can be divided into two sections. The first section is a plea for help and conveys David's emotional and physical needs. The second section is his response to those needs. The first verse sets the tone for the rest: "Come with great power, O God, and rescue me! Defend me with your might" (Ps 54:1).

David realizes that, although he has a small army around him, if Saul were ever to find him and engage him in war, he and his men would not survive. David's six hundred misfits were no match for Saul's three thousand of Israel's finest. Thus, David had to trust in a fragile and delicate game of cat and mouse, where Saul could never pinpoint his location. David goes on to pray: "Listen to my prayer, O God. Pay attention to my plea. For strangers are attacking me; violent people are trying to kill me. They care nothing for God" (vv 2–3).

Have you ever been in a situation where you felt you had no control over the outcome? It's frustrating. It makes you feel useless and completely powerless. That's how David felt in his situation.

It's interesting how God works and prepares us for the future. Even before Saul again came after David, this week we learned about a strange interaction he had with the house of Nabal. Because of the proactive and godly Abigail, David was spared from defending himself and shedding innocent blood. No wonder, when it came to the encounter with Saul, David felt compelled to pray: "Defend me with *your* might."

Once again, David learned he had no need to defend himself. It is a lesson we all need to learn. Why? Because God can't defend us when we defend ourselves. You notice it was only after David chose not to destroy Nabal that God struck down the wicked man. David then chose to spare Saul's life and place him in the hands of God—his defender.

What are you doing to defend yourself instead of placing the situation in the hands of God? We would be wise to learn from David, a man after God's own heart, in dealing with conflict. Instead of defending ourselves, why not put God in charge. I've found He's much more capable at winning than I am. Read the second half of Psalm 54 and declare it:

> But God is my helper. The Lord keeps me alive! May the evil plans of my enemies be turned against them. Do as You promised and put an end to them. I will sacrifice a voluntary offering to You; I will praise Your name, O Lord, for it is good. For You have rescued me from my troubles and helped me to triumph over my enemies (vv 4–7).

One phrase that stands out is "voluntary offering." Remember, any time we choose to make God our defender, we do so voluntarily. Could that voluntary offering (of not defending ourselves) be the key to deliverance from our troubles and enemies?

WEEK 8
HIDING AMONG ENEMIES

DAY 50: MONDAY
1 SAMUEL 27:2–12; 29:1–30:4

For almost ten years, David waited, day after day, with similar results. Each year that passed seemed a little more depressing than the last. Even as he, his wives, and his men rode into Gath of Philistia, of all places, it seemed surreal.

David remembered how he had left the province years earlier—all alone. He had been thrown out of the king's court after pretending to be insane. Then, he was on his own; now, he had six hundred men and their families traveling with him. Upon arriving and requesting a meeting with the king of Gath, he felt a little queasy in his stomach. *So much has changed and not for the good*, David couldn't help but think.

Surprisingly, King Achish was delighted to receive David and his men. After years of being rejected, it was nice to be welcomed for a change. David scoffed to himself: *My enemy welcomes me more than my own kin.*

Before long, David was given the city of Ziklag in which to settle. King Achish frequently sent him out to fight against Israel. David and his men, however, tricked the king. Instead they raided the Geshurites, the Girzites, and the Amalekites, bringing back much plunder. They were sure to kill every living survivor so no word would get back to the Achish.

In fact, when the king asked where David's raid had taken place, David answered, "Against the south of Judah, the Jerahmeelites, and the Kenites" (1 Sam 27:10).

Achish believed what David said and thought, *"By now the people of Israel must hate him bitterly. Now he will have to stay here and serve me forever!"* (1 Sam 27:12).

After a year and four months of this, all of Philistia rallied its forces against Israel. The Philistine army gathered in Aphek to meet the Israelite army which camped at Jezreel.

David had been in many a battle like this except he used to be on the opposite side. *Surely they haven't forgotten when I was a boy and fought against their champion Goliath years early.* It was weird to picture himself on this side of the battle—fighting *for* the Philistines. But he readied himself to do so.

When the rulers of the Philistines marched their troops, David and his men marched behind them with King Achish. But the Philistine leaders wanted to know what the Hebrews were doing among them. They asked, "What are these Hebrews doing here? . . . Isn't this the same David about whom the women of Israel sing in their dances, 'Saul has killed his thousands, and David his ten thousands'?" (1 Sam. 29:3–5).

King Achish called David over and said to him, "I think you should go with me into battle, for I've never found a single flaw in you from the day you arrived until today. But the other Philistine rulers won't hear of it. Please don't upset them, but go back quietly" (1 Sam. 28:6–7).

David pretended to complain about it, but secretly thought, *Whew! Thanks, God.* David had no idea how he would ever live past the report of fighting against his own nation. "God really spared us this time," David rejoiced to his men on the way home.

Three days later, the rejoicing was over. That sense of uneasiness was back in the pit of his stomach. Far from the city of Ziklag, David saw smoke rising. As they drew closer, he and his men realized they had been raided by the Amalekites. Upon arriving, they learned that every possession, including David's two wives, Abigail and Ahinoam, had been captured, along with all the families and possessions belonging to his men.

David had experienced some lows before, but this seemed unbearable. He and his men wept until no more tears came.

DAY 51: TUESDAY
1 SAMUEL 30:6; PSALM 18:27–29, 32–36

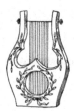

As if returning to Ziklag without the taste of battle wasn't enough, this blow to David and his men was most severe. Distraught, David left his men and went to his house to contemplate what to do. On his way, he overheard someone say, "We should have never gone to fight with the Philistines."

"We shouldn't even be here in Gath in the first place," another warrior replied.

David soon arrived at his house. It was a pile of ruins. The Amalekites had burned it to the ground. The words of his warriors still in his thoughts, he started to question himself, *Are they right? Have I led them astray?*

Abishai suddenly arrived unannounced and asked to speak to him privately. His personal visit could only mean one thing. "My Lord, everyone is talking of stoning you."

Really? David didn't respond.

"My lord, we can't just sit here on our hands and do nothing. We must go and reclaim what is rightfully ours."

Maybe their stoning me would be for the best, David pondered. *At least it would put an end to my misery.* "I know," David said. This news felt like a knock-out blow to his spirit. In that moment, David wondered, *If not my men, who can I really trust?*

All at once, David had a startling revelation—*I've put too much faith in those around me.* He thought back to the cave of Adullam. He had been so delighted when men started arriving. How encouraging it had been to have had support—finally. And he was in good company, many being outlaws. *I've put my hope in the wrong place,* David sighed in disgust. If after all this time and all they had been through together they still doubted him, there was only one place he could go to find security. *God, You are my only hope!*

"Get me Abiathar," David commanded Abishai. "And tell him to bring the linen ephod to inquire of the Lord for me."

After dismissing his commander, David fell to the floor in despair. He tried not to dwell on his wives being in the hands of a heathen army, but he couldn't help it. Rage welled up in his heart, and all he wanted to do was punch something or kill someone!

The moment of betrayal by his men was the deepest wounding he had ever felt. For the first time in a long time, David was afraid, scared, and alone. There was but one place to go in a time like this; he found strength in the Lord.

Out of the deepest place of his being, he cried,

> To the faithful You show Yourself faithful, to the blameless You show Yourself blameless, to the pure You show Yourself pure . . . You save the humble. . . . For who is God besides the Lord? And who is the Rock except our God? It is God who arms me with strength and keeps my way secure. He makes my feet like the feet of a deer. . . . He trains my hands for battle; my arms can bend a bow of bronze. You make Your saving help my shield, and Your right hand sustains me. . . . You provide a broad path for my feet, so that my ankles do not give way (Ps 18:25–27, 31–36 NIV).

DAY 52: WEDNESDAY
1 SAMUEL 30:8–30; 2 SAMUEL 1:2–4

Abiathar, the priest, arrived with the sacred ephod. David asked the Lord if he should go after the raiders and if he would overtake them. The Lord said, "Yes, go after them. You will surely recover everything that was taken from you!" (1 Sam 30:8).

David raced after the Amalekites and got as far as the brook Besor. Many of his men were too exhausted to cross it. David and only four hundred of the six hundred men continued in hot pursuit.

David knew he would be outnumbered, but that was normal. With the word from God in his heart, he and his men set out confidently. When they found the Amalekites, the raiding party was drinking and celebrating because of the great amount of plunder it had captured. David and his men charged in on them, killing them through the night and the next day until evening. By the end of it all, only four hundred young Amalekite males, who had camels, had escaped the onslaught. David and his men took their wives, their stuff, and their sons and daughters back. They recovered everything —even their flocks, herds, and other livestock. And as they were returning with all their possessions intact, driving the cattle homeward, David's men said, "This plunder belongs to David!" (1 Sam 30:20).

After returning to Besor Valley, the two hundred who stayed back met them with joy. Some of the troublemakers in the returning group didn't want to share the plunder, but David quickly nipped that in the bud. "We share everything with all—those who fought and those who didn't have the strength to fight," he commanded, and no one objected. This attitude of generosity became an unwritten policy from that day on. David modeled this by sharing with the elders of Judah, sending a great amount of plunder to Bethel, Hebron, and all the other places he and his men visited from time to time.

David praised the Lord out of joy and thanksgiving, singing, "I love you, Lord, my strength. The Lord is my rock, my fortress and my deliverer; my God is my rock, in whom I take refuge, my shield and the horn of my salvation, my stronghold" (Ps 18:1–2 NIV).

He paused after remembering his prayer a few days earlier; how downcast and depressed he had been. In celebration, David cried,

> In my distress I called to the Lord; I cried to my God for help. From His temple He heard my voice; my cry came before Him, into His ears. . . . I pursued my enemies and overtook them; I did not turn back till they were destroyed. I crushed them so that they could not rise; they fell beneath my feet. You armed me with strength for battle; You humbled my adversaries before me. You made my enemies turn their backs in flight, and I destroyed my foes (Ps 18:6, 37–40 NIV).

DAY 53: THURSDAY
2 SAMUEL 1:2–15

Three days after their victory, while David and his men were resting, a messenger from Saul's army arrived with some troubling news. The messenger's clothes were ripped and his head covered in dirt to show that he was in mourning. He fell to David's feet in respect.

David asked him, "Where have you come from?" (2 Sam 2:3).

"I escaped from the Israelite camp" (2 Sam 2:3) he said. "Our entire army fled from the battle. Many of the men are dead, and Saul and his son Jonathan are also dead" (2 Sam 2:4).

David wasn't sure how to feel at first. Yes, Saul had been very evil toward him, but he was still king. But Jonathan, to hear of his death was overwhelming. *Oh Jonathan!* David lamented. *My friend and my brother is dead!*

It was more than that. The wound inside him went far beyond the death of a king and his son and closest friend. David's pain stemmed from a deep responsibility to God's people. Although in a different circumstance, it was the same feeling he had when Goliath lifted his terrorizing voice in defiance of God and the armies of Israel.

For some reason, David's mind went back to his shepherding days. When the shepherd was struck down, ill, or absent, the sheep scattered. This current state of Israel was troubling. David wailed loudly in the presence of his men. He tore his clothes, put ashes on his head, and wept for Israel. Deep-seated compassion for how far they had fallen gripped his heart, leaving him breathless. And when he thought about Jonathan, the agony felt like more than he could bear.

As he lay there, in anguish, he couldn't help but think: *Saul—the king—is dead.* His closest confidant, the king's son, and the next in line, had also fallen. Samuel had prophesied David would be the next king. It was hard not to let his mind go there: *Is this the time? Will I finally become king?*

David chided himself for having such a thought. The king and his son hadn't even been buried properly. Something else troubled him. *I wonder why the messenger did not stay and protect the king?* Something didn't add up.

"How did you get away after Saul's death?" David asked the man.

"Saul was wounded and knew he wasn't going to escape when he called me over to him just before he died," the man replied.

David was alarmed at his response. "So, what did you do?"

In a nervous tone, the messenger explained, "He told me to strike him down, and at his request, well, I did."

"Kill him!" David told one of his men. "His own words condemn him. Strike him down for laying a hand against the Lord's anointed."

Then, one of the young men from his ranks struck him down, and the bearer of Saul's and Jonathan's deaths was slain.

DAY 54: FRIDAY
2 SAMUEL 2:1–27

After inquiring of the Lord, David went up from Gath into Judah, to the city of Hebron. And settling there, the men of the region came to David and anointed him king over Judah.

It was a joyous occasion yet bittersweet as all Israel was in mourning for their fallen king. After being anointed by the prophet Samuel almost a decade earlier, it appeared things had finally lined up in David's favor. He knew his destiny, but how would he unite the kingdom? If Judah had already anointed him king, certainly all Israel would follow suit.

Now, king of Judah, David contemplated and devised a way to honor the former king and his son. "What better way to remember their lives than a song," he told his citizens and then required they learn the lyrics and melody. The song became known as the "Song of the Bow." In the presence of the elders of Judah and his men, David sang:

Your pride and joy, O Israel, lies dead on the hills! Oh, how the mighty heroes have fallen! . . . The bow of Jonathan was powerful, and the sword of Saul did its mighty work. They shed the blood of their enemies and pierced the bodies of mighty heroes. How beloved and gracious were Saul and Jonathan! They were together in life and in death. They were swifter than eagles, stronger than lions. O women of Israel, weep for Saul, for he dressed you in luxurious scarlet clothing, in garments decorated with gold. Oh, how the mighty heroes have fallen in battle! Jonathan lies dead on the hills. How I weep for you, my brother Jonathan! Oh, how much I loved you! And your love for me was deep, deeper than the love of women! Oh, how the mighty heroes have fallen! (2 Sam 2:19, 22–27).

The elders looked delighted, but David's men were another story. Their faces told it all—exactly what they were thinking.

Later, Abishai confirmed it. "That was quite a song, my King."

"Your sarcasm is duly noted," David replied.

"Gracious heroes, the pride of Israel," Abishai said, rolling his eyes. "Jonathan, yes, but Saul?"

David put his hand on his commander's shoulder. "I know how Saul treated us. I was there, along with you."

"He was a madman in all respects of the word. And his relentless pursuit of your demise drove him there. I just don't understand."

"I know," David said. "But we must honor the good he has done. He unified Israel and fought on Israel's behalf. And before he changed, remember that he was God's choice."

David could tell Abishai was listening even though the commander didn't respond.

"You've heard me say it time and time again, and it would be good for you—and the men—to remember that he *was* the Lord's anointed servant."

DAY 55: SATURDAY
REFLECTIONS FROM THE WEEK

It is hard to look at the life of David without considering its similarity to the life Christ. David was a man after God's own heart, that we know for sure. Would Christ Jesus in the flesh be any less a man after God's own heart? No, much more so, in fact.

Since David was so far ahead of his time, like Jesus, many of the things he did made no sense to the people around him. I'm sure David's rag-tag army of misfits must have rolled their eyes on more than one occasion. His passion and reckless pursuit of pleasing God and not man were so foreign to them that, many times, they didn't know how to react. Doesn't that sound familiar to Jesus' earthly ministry?

In truth, Saul was David's enemy. We know the relationship was complicated because Jonathan was caught in the middle. But that doesn't negate the fact that David felt genuine pain from both their deaths. The song he wrote in their honor tells the true story. He calls them *heroes*. He calls them *mighty warriors*. He encouraged all Israel to weep and mourn for them. He praised their accomplishments, even as misguided as they were sometimes.

David likely received a similar response to what the Son of Man did when He said, "But to you who are willing to listen, I say, love your enemies! Do good to those who hate you. Bless those who curse you. Pray for those who hurt you" (Luke 6:27).

Centuries later, Jesus taught us how to gauge the true measure of a man: by his fruit, by his love. What Jesus was calling us to was a love, not for those who are nice to us, but for those who oppose us, persecute us, and abuse us out of spite.

I find it interesting that David, the precursor to the Messiah (the ultimate example of a man after God's own heart), instinctively reacted in the same manner as Jesus did. He loved his enemies. As Jesus did in front of His disciples, David modeled this in front of his mighty men and all Israel by extending honor and acclaim to those who persecuted him.

What was the response? The disciples changed the known world. And in David's case, his men followed his example by tearing their clothes, putting ashes on their heads, and, perhaps, even singing the song about the crazy king who tried to kill their leader. David, a man after God's heart, was teaching them Christian principles before Christ. Astonishing!

David's understanding of kingdom principles and conduct was remarkable, especially given the fact Israel had only crowned one king up to this point. David realized conducting himself as king had less to do with conquering territories, maintaining order, or instituting law and more to do with serving in love, honor, and respect. In David's mind, that was the Kingdom of God. It wasn't a title, sitting on a throne, or notoriety.

I find this worth noting and even more admirable than David's ascent to the throne. I guess what I'm saying is: Before David ever became a king, he not only knew the King of kings; he acted like Him.

Oh, that we could be so in love with the King of kings that we would do the same. Perhaps, like David, if we did, the church would look and operate more like a Kingdom rather than a religious establishment.

DAY 56: SUNDAY
A CLOSER LOOK AT PSALM 18

Considering all David endured, I find the following statement fascinating: "God's way is perfect. All the Lord's promises prove true. He is a shield for all who look to Him for protection. For who is God except the Lord? Who but our God is a solid rock?" (Ps 18:30–31).

God's ways are perfect? Really, David? Even running for your life from Saul? Even fighting incognito while wearing a Philistine uniform? Even when your family and possessions are stolen by a band of heathen Amalekites? Yes, even then. David not only believed what he said in Psalm 18, but he also lived it!

And although David had a small army of brave warriors around him, he eventually realized they were no help to him, that is, without the help of the Lord his God. We learn this when his men contemplated stoning him at Ziklag.

David went on to pen some of my favorite verses from the Psalms: "God arms me with strength, and He makes my way perfect. He makes me as surefooted as a deer, enabling me to stand on mountain heights. He trains my hands for battle; He strengthens my arm to draw a bronze bow" (Ps 18:32–34).

What great imagery! First off, David compares himself to a sure-footed deer standing on the heights. Any hunter knows that deer are easy prey—defenseless—except for the fact they are incredibly elusive. In almost every case, David and his small band of warriors were greatly outnumbered. In fact, had they encountered Saul or a heathen nation's vast army head-on, they could have been easily overtaken.

Whether avoiding Saul or fighting the Amalekites to recapture their wives and children, it was only by God's enablement and empowerment that David gained the upper hand in every battle. David's vigilant dependence upon God was the only reason he always prevailed.

I'm reminded of Jeremiah's frequent description of God as the *Lord God of Heaven's armies* (see Jer 19:15; 44:25). David, a great military commander in his own right, trusted in the same God Jeremiah described. In New Testament vernacular, David understood his struggle was not against flesh and blood, but against supernatural forces in high places (see Eph 16:12). And for that, he needed much more than military strategy. He needed God, his solid Rock!

Along with David's elusiveness (as a deer), secondly, in verse 34, he declares: "He trains my hands for battle; my arms can bend a bow of bronze" (NIV). In human strength, it is impossible to bend a bow made of bronze. And yet, David knew God's Spirit would give him the power to do just that—the impossible.

How could David make such claims so confidently? Perhaps because he constantly found himself in situations where, without God's help, it seemed hopeless. I seriously doubt David had a bow made of bronze. In reality, he was actually saying, "Even if I had to bend bronze, jump a mountain, leap off a cliff, run through an entire troop, or kill a giant [which he did], I could!" And yes, he could, because the Lord was with him. The sure-footed words of Jesus ring true: "Humanly speaking, it is impossible. But with God everything is possible" (Matt 29:26).

What battle are you facing that seems impossible? Take a lesson from David. Let God train your hands for battle, realizing it is not a struggle of flesh but Spirit. Read and declare these powerful truths about God's enablement in dire situations:

> I love You, Lord; You are my strength. The Lord is my rock, my fortress, and my savior; my God is my rock, in whom I find protection. He is my shield, the power that saves me, and my place of safety. I called on the Lord, who is worthy of praise, and He saved me from my enemies. . . . You rescue the humble, but You humiliate the proud. You light a lamp for me. The Lord, my God, lights up my darkness. In your strength I can crush an army; with my God I can scale any wall. . . . God arms me with strength, and He makes my way perfect. He makes me as surefooted as a deer, enabling me to stand on mountain heights. He trains my hands for battle; He strengthens my arm to draw a bronze bow (Ps 18:1–3, 27–29, 32–34).

WEEK 9
FROM PASTURE TO PALACE

DAY 57: MONDAY
2 SAMUEL 2:4–13

When David received word that men of Jabesh-gilead had buried Saul, he decided to send this message:

May the Lord bless you for being so loyal to your master Saul and giving him a decent burial. May the Lord be loyal to you in return and reward you with his unfailing love! And I, too, will reward you for what you have done. Now that Saul is dead, I ask you to be my strong and loyal subjects like the people of Judah, who have anointed me as their new king (2 Sam 2:5–7).

David knew the wound was fresh. He also knew Saul had many loyal subjects. Even as he sent the message, David wondered how they would respond. He waited patiently for a reply; he watched closely for an arriving entourage—perhaps even an approaching army. Days came and went. Weeks passed, but no one arrived. Nobody came. "What does this mean?" David asked the Lord.

"Surely all Israel knew of Samuel's prophecy; I was clearly God's choice."

Finally, word reached the king of Judah, "Abner son of Ner, commander of Saul's army, has anointed Ishbosheth, Saul's son, king of Israel."

"I knew it," David vented to his men. "I knew Saul had turned the hearts of Israel away from me."

The lines were drawn: Israel with Ishbosheth who ruled from Mahanaim, and Judah who remained loyal to David and ruled from Hebron.

Israel's decision was a blow David had not prepared for. He was more than disappointed to be rejected. And yet, rejection by a people he loved so dearly seemed to be his lot in life. As always, David found hope and encouragement in the Lord his God and determined to rule faithfully and justly over the single tribe of Judah.

It wasn't all bad; there was good news as well. His nephew Joab, a brilliant military commander, came to him and finally agreed to be the general of Judah's army. It was a good thing. After rejecting David as king, Abner roused Ishbosheth's troops to wage war with Judah. Joab responded by leading David's army out to face them head-on at the pool of Gibeon. Just one generation after their first king was crowned, the kingdom of Israel had already erupted in civil war.

David peered out over the countryside of Gibeon, and the two armies camped across from each other. Although it reminded him of the day he defeated Goliath, this just felt weird. Across the way was no heathen nation. It was *his* nation—*his* people. No, *God's* people—*God's* nation.

And yet, here they sat. It appeared Saul's son was following in his father's footsteps. David knew there was only one reason

Ishbosheth had rallied the troop—*To get back at me*, he was convinced. It made his heart hurt.

DAY 58: TUESDAY
2 SAMUEL 2:14–17

Nobody moved. Nobody could, at least not yet. It was a good, old-fashioned stand-off. David wasn't the only one feeling mixed emotions; everyone felt it. This was no heathen army. These were Hebrew brothers whom they had celebrated festivals and Passovers with. They had offered burnt sacrifices together—and feasted together.

Nobody knew what to do. "Are we really going to war against our kin?" was all the chatter.

David knew what he felt, but wondered if Ishbosheth was crazy enough to actually attack. *Are we really going to do this?* David wasn't sure.

Abner offered this suggestion to Joab, "Let's have a few of our warriors fight hand to hand here in front of us" (2 Sam 2:14).

Joab agreed, and twelve men from each side were selected to fight—twelve men from Ishbosheth and twelve from David.

Snickers and sneers could be heard from both sides. It appeared the battle was turning into a schoolyard brawl. Abner's request seemed plausible, and, in essence, was easing the two armies into battle. David knew it was no coincidence the number twelve had been chosen. Abner was slick. He was pining for war and making a point. By asking twelve men from eleven tribes of Israel against the one tribe of Judah, he made sure Judah knew the odds. As the twenty-four men faced each other and began fighting, something remarkable happened. Each of the twelve struck the other while being killed at the same time. All twenty-four fell—and quickly.

David stood to his feet, as did Ishbosheth. At that moment, it was crystal clear to David; he knew God had given both sides the same results—death. It was almost as if God were saying, "No good is going to come out of killing your kin. It's only going to end badly —for both sides." David understood, but did Ishbosheth?

Evidently not because an intense battle ensued, resulting in the defeat of Abner and the men of Israel. David's men of Judah defeated their brethren.

He's just like his father, David agonized. Saul had always been bent on retaining power and control, no matter what the cost. It appeared Ishbosheth was no different. *Oh, Jonathan, if you had lived, things would be different.*

DAY 59: WEDNESDAY
2 SAMUEL 2:18–3:1

As Israel's army began suffering heavy losses at the hand of Judah, they ran in fear. Asahel, the fastest of Judah's runners, relentlessly pursued Abner.

"Get away from me—I don't want to kill you!" Abner shouted back to him. "How could I ever face Joab?"

Asahel refused to retreat and Abner was forced to kill him. It was the most of horrific of deaths; he thrust the butt end of his spear through Asahel's stomach and the spear came out through his back.

When Joab and Abishai heard the news, they chased Abner vehemently but were forced to give up at the hill of Ammah near Giah when the sun went down. After counting the casualties, Joab discovered that only nineteen men were missing apart from Asahel, but three hundred and sixty of Israel's men fell. In anguish, Joab buried his brother's body in Bethlehem before returning to Judah.

"That was the beginning of a long war between those who were loyal to Saul and those loyal to David. As time passed David became stronger and stronger, while Saul's dynasty became weaker and weaker" (2 Sam 3:1).

As David grew in power, he also grew more unsettled. His heart broke every time there was a dispute between Judah and his fellow countrymen. "This is not how it's supposed to be," he lamented to God in prayer. One day, David asked himself a question: *What do I want more than anything else?*

As far as David remembered, when Samuel anointed him king, it was not over the single tribe of Judah but over all Israel. *Is that really what I want? To be king?* His initial response was troubling. He had always said having God's presence was enough. Now that he was king over one tribe—not twelve—he wasn't so sure. In that moment, David realized how deceiving and wicked his heart could be. Grabbing his harp, he cried out to the Lord: "O Lord, You have examined my heart and know everything about me. You know when I sit down or stand up. You know my thoughts even when I'm far away" (Ps 139:1–2).

What an interesting song, David thought. A little scary, but what came out next scared him more: "Search me, O God, and know my heart; test me and know my anxious thoughts. Point out anything in me that offends You, and lead me along the path of everlasting life" (Ps 139:23–24).

David threw his harp to the side and listened with all his might. "So, I guess I'm asking You," David prayed with a lump in his throat. "What do I *really* want, Lord? You know better than I. So please show me."

DAY 60: THURSDAY
2 SAMUEL 3:2–29

As kings do, David began having children. He took a number of wives in addition to Abigail, the widow of Nabal, and Ahinoam from Jezreel. During his reign over Judah, in all, he had six children by six different wives and concubines.

One day, messengers arrived from Israel with a message for the king. Surprisingly, it was from Abner, who said, "Doesn't the entire land belong to you? Make a solemn pact with me, and I will help turn over all of Israel to you" (2 Sam 3:12).

David couldn't believe his ears. Was it a trap? David didn't think so. So he agreed but with one stipulation: "I will not negotiate with you unless you bring back my wife Michal, Saul's daughter, when you come" (2 Sam 3:13). David thought, *We'll see if he means business.*

Sure enough, when Abner arrived at a feast David prepared in his honor, Michal was with him. David was thrilled and knew the Israeli general was serious. He also realized that Abner was probably the only hope to unite the two kingdoms back together. The people respected him and were not only willing to follow him into battle, but would receive his wise counsel. *Enough to overthrow Ishbosheth, the son of Saul?* David wondered. With Abner's help, maybe.

At the feast, Abner later requested, "Let me go and call an assembly of all Israel to support my lord the king. They will make a covenant with you to make you their king, and you will rule over everything your heart desires" (2 Sam 3:21).

David granted him safe passage.

Everything appeared to be lining up—*finally!* Had David known how long and difficult the journey, he would have told Samuel, "No. Not me. I'm not the right man for the job." Did he really have a choice, though? He was just a boy all those years ago when the prophet showed up in town. For over a decade he had held onto Samuel's words, even after the prophet's death. And now, based on this meeting with Abner, it was plausible. It wasn't a dream or speculation anymore. It was a true, concrete possibility.

David went to bed with his wife Michal that night, thoughts swimming in his head. There was so much he wanted to talk about. She had an inside perspective no one else did. It was weird. She was different. *Of course, she's different*, David decided. She had been forced to marry another man. No doubt, for years, Michal had been poisoned with lies about David. But she had loved him once. *Does she still?* David believed she did.

In the wee hours of the morning, a messenger stirred David awake. David jumped. "What is it? What's happened?"

"It's Abner, sir," the messenger replied. "Joab and Abishai have murdered Abner to avenge the death of their brother."

David's heart sank. "What? When?"

"After leaving the feast, my King, they followed him and killed him."

David leapt from his bed and paced the floor, distraught. In anger, he avowed by the Lord,

I and my kingdom are forever innocent of this crime against Abner son of Ner. Joab and his family are the guilty ones. May the family of Joab be cursed in every generation with a man who has open sores or leprosy or who walks on crutches or dies by the sword or begs for food! (2 Sam 3:28–29).

That night, in one fatal act, which David was unaware, his newly formed alliance went up in smoke. *Poof! Gone!* After dismissing the messenger, David collapsed on his bed. He once again cursed the name of Joab and Abishai. He had never been so angry at anyone. *How will the people of Israel believe I had nothing to do with this?* He fumed. It was a hard sell in the first place; without The question he had been stewing over for months returned: *What do I want more than anything?* Was it to be king? God had remained silent without the hint of an answer until David heard Him ask, "So what if you don't become king? Ever?"

David rolled over and put his face in his hands. Tears filled his eyes. "You alone know, Lord. More important than becoming king, I want to please you—really please you! Be my shepherd, and I will obey you—always!" His voice trembled as he prayed through the sobs, "And yes, even if that means that I never become king."

DAY 61: FRIDAY
2 SAMUEL 3:31–5:5

David was far too riled up to sleep, so he lay there. In the stillness of dawn, God revealed to him exactly what to do. But it was more than an action, something more important had happened, something deep in his heart. As he rose from bed to face a very troubling situation, he felt light on his feet and confident in his ability to react.

David sent for Joab and Abishai, and commanded them, "Tear your clothes and put on burlap. Mourn for Abner" (2 Sam 3:31). David himself walked behind the funeral procession. In mourning, he refused to eat. It wasn't an act, but sincere and genuine, and the people knew it. This act endeared him to the people, and everyone in Judah and all of Israel realized David wasn't responsible for the murder of Abner.

With Abner's death, Ishbosheth did his best to hold things together but ended up getting assassinated by two of his captains. They cut off his head and brought it to King David announcing, "Here is the head of Ishbosheth, the son of your enemy Saul who tried to kill you. Today the Lord has given my lord the king revenge on Saul and his entire family!" (2 Sam 4:8).

David couldn't figure out why someone announcing they had killed one of Saul's relatives was good news. "How dare you lift a hand against the Lord's anointed! Shouldn't I hold you responsible for his blood and rid the earth of you?" he told them. Then he had them killed.

Israel was left in shambles, and for five years the nation floundered like sheep without a shepherd. David, however, didn't interfere. He waited patiently and faithfully led and served the tribe of Judah. And finally, the Lord intervened, when, after a decade and a half since Samuel's prophecy, David looked out across the plains of Hebron and saw the coming entourage of Israeli elders far off in the distance.

Then, David heard God's familiar voice again, "What do you want more than anything else?"

"Unity!" David replied. "Unity between you and me, Lord. And unity among all God's people!" David sensed the Lord's pleasure in his answer. So he rose and went out to greet the arriving caravan.

The elders of Israel greeted him warmly and said, "We are your own flesh and blood. In the past, when Saul was our king, you were the one who really led the forces of Israel. And the Lord told you, 'You will be the shepherd of my people Israel. You will be Israel's leader'" (2 Sam 5:1–2). With that, David made a covenant with the elders there at Hebron. They anointed him as king of Israel.

In celebration that night, David sang and worshiped before all Judah and Israel:

> How wonderful and pleasant it is when brothers live together in harmony! For harmony is as precious as the anointing oil that was poured over Aaron's head, that ran down his beard and onto the

border of his robe. . . . And there the Lord has pronounced His blessing, even life everlasting (Ps 133).

David had finally arrived; the prophecy was fulfilled. The anointed teen and giant slayer who had spent years on the run from Saul was now king of Israel. Israel's Shepherd King was thirty years old when he began to reign, and he reigned a total of forty years, seven-and-a-half years in Judah and thirty-three years over all Israel.

DAY 62: SATURDAY
REFLECTIONS FROM THE WEEK

There's one task I really enjoy doing: cleaning the garage. Here's a task I don't enjoy doing: mowing the grass. Why? When I clean the garage, it's done, and I know I won't have to touch it for another few months. Why do I hate mowing the grass? It's simple: after it's mowed, less than a week later it's overgrown again. It requires constant attention and upkeep.

If you're like me, I enjoy projects, such as writing books, that have a concrete beginning and end, a starting point and finish line. When they are done, they're done, and I don't have to think about them anymore. Unfortunately, in my experience, I've found many of the ways God operates are much more like mowing the grass than cleaning the garage.

I can't think of a better example than a short verse in this week's reading. It's so short, in fact, that you may have missed it: "That was the beginning of a long war between those who were loyal to Saul and those loyal to David. As time passed David became stronger and stronger, while Saul's dynasty became weaker and weaker" (2 Sam 3:1).

After being crowned king in Judah, in haste, David sends a message to Israel, asking for its loyalty, only to find out Ishbosheth has been crowned king. Can you imagine David's frustration? Just when the finish line was in sight, David was rejected again. And this rejection went much deeper than any previous rejection he suffered.

While he was on the run, I believe there was a side of David that blamed everything on Saul. And why not? It was obvious that Saul was jealous. David wasn't unaware of the songs being sung about his victories over "tens of thousands" as opposed to Saul's "thousands." Besides, Saul was the reason he was on the run in the first place. Saul hunted him down. And Saul tried to kill him multiple times. Saul, Saul, Saul. It was all Saul's fault.

With that in mind, after Saul's and Jonathan's deaths, David assumed the kingdom was his. What a crushing blow when David gets Israel's answer. David realized: *Maybe it wasn't just Saul who was against me but the entire nation.* It's one thing to be rejected by a crazy king who was threatened by you. It's quite another to be rejected by an entire nation of your kin.

David didn't fall apart, however. And, quite remarkably, he didn't try to take the kingdom by force. You notice it was Abner and Ishbosheth that waged war on Judah, not the other way around. Joab and David merely led the troops out in defense of their territory, and God gave them the victory.

It was after that victory where the tiny verse appears: "That was the beginning of a long war between those who were loyal to Saul and those loyal to David. As time passed David became stronger and stronger, while Saul's dynasty became weaker and weaker" (2 Sam 3:1).

When you read this verse, can you picture the progression? David grew *stronger and stronger* while Saul grew *weaker and weaker*. David's rise to the throne didn't happen *suddenly*; it happened *progressively*. Maybe you've heard, as I have, sermons describing God as a "suddenly God." And yes, countless passages are ascribed to God's moving "suddenly." But in most cases, there's usually a backstory.

I heard one well-known and highly acclaimed ministry leader describe how he rose to influence in the body of Christ. He said, "When people started to take notice of my ministry, I did the same thing I'd been doing for thirty years." He went on to say, "I guess you could say, 'I'm a thirty-year overnight success.'" How well this statement describes David's rise to power.

When David did become king, it was his "suddenly" moment. He had arrived at his destiny, and what had been spoken over the teenager by Samuel finally came to pass. But I think you'll agree, it was a long journey getting there. And what do we learn from his life during those years?

First, it was very hard. David was given ample opportunity to give up, but he didn't. He was rejected but kept his heart pure before God, even to the point of showing honor to his enemies (those he deemed as "God's anointed.") Lastly, we learn that David held to an incredible and relentless pursuit of God's presence during the process.

We could describe David as follows: David was not a king who liked to worship; David was a worshiper who became king.

DAY 63: SUNDAY
A CLOSER LOOK AT PSALM 139

I absolutely love Psalm 139. Through the years, it has become very dear to me. In it, David penned some of his most intimate experiences with God. Consider the following passage:

> You saw me before I was born. Every day of my life was recorded in Your book. Every moment was laid out before a single day had passed. How precious are Your thoughts about me, O God. They cannot be numbered! I can't even count them; they outnumber the grains of sand! (Ps 139:16–18).

How fascinating! To what book was David referring? Was he speaking about the Bible or the Book of Life written about in Revelation? One thing is certain: David knew his actions, and even his worship mattered to God. It was being recorded or, based on his terminology, prerecorded.

Given his difficult journey, it's not hard to imagine how these lyrics must have brought incredible strength to his spirit. David developed intimacy with God (even before the world knew it had need of a Messiah) that rivals those of us today who enjoy a new covenant based on better promises.

I wonder how many grains of sand *are* on Planet Earth. We could only guess. I'm sure David didn't know. Like David, we could only answer: innumerable, infinite. Yet David understood how often and dearly God thought about him. Incredible!

I love the aforementioned passage, but it's not nearly as breathtaking to me as the last verses of the Psalm: "Search me, O God, and know my heart; test me and know my anxious thoughts. Point out anything in me that offends You, and lead me along the path of everlasting life" (vv 23–24).

By speaking in terms never before heard (and well before their time), David, the forerunner, did it again. Today, we take full advantage of the entirety of Scripture. David didn't have this luxury. His writings were real, raw, and sometimes crude. When I say crude, what I mean is a passage such as this, "O God, if only You would destroy the wicked! Get out of my life, you murderers! . . . O Lord, shouldn't I hate those who hate You? Shouldn't I despise those who oppose You? Yes, I hate them with total hatred, for Your enemies are my enemies" (Ps 139:19, 21–22). It doesn't get any more crude than telling God, "Kill them! I totally hate them, so kill them all!" It was raw; it was also honest and sincere.

And God loved it.

And remember, David had no idea his worship songs would be canonized. He simply poured out his heart to God. And, at some point, perhaps during the writing of this Psalm, he realized: *My heart is easily led astray. And because of that fact, I could easily be deceived.* Deception of the heart is tricky because in your heart you think you're right when all along you are wrong. It's interesting that David made this discovery.

The reason this is interesting is because it wasn't until centuries later that Jeremiah described the heart as, "deceitful above all things and beyond cure. Who can understand it?" (Jer 17:9). David's wise son, Solomon, must have learned this lesson from his father for he wrote, "Guard your heart above all else, for it determines the course of your life," and, "Many are the plans in a person's heart, but it is the Lord's purpose that prevails" (Prov 4:23; 19:21).

If David understood this, what was his answer? It's simple. David took the matter to the Lord, and said, "God, since I can't understand what's going on in my heart, I need You to show me. I lay my heart open before You and promise not to be defensive. I'm not going to justify my selfish ambitions, my own agendas, or haughty tendencies. Here's my heart, laid bare—search it!"

Have you ever been courageous enough to do this? The first time I was, it scared me to death. I've never been more nervous or embarrassed.

As I've discovered, laying your heart bare before God is a price many are unwilling to pay. And yet, there's no greater reward. Oh, yes, you may not like what God says. I'm sure David wrestled with God's findings. And yet, I believe this verse, more than any other, is why he was a man after God's own heart. Read and declare this incredible Psalm:

> O Lord, you have examined my heart and know everything about me. You know when I sit down or stand up. You know my thoughts even when I'm far away. . . . I can never escape from Your Spirit! I can never get away from Your presence! If I go up to heaven, You are there; if I go down to the grave, You are there. If I ride the wings of the morning, if I dwell by the farthest oceans, even there Your hand will guide me, and Your strength will support me. How precious are Your thoughts about me, O God. They cannot be

numbered! I can't even count them; they outnumber the grains of sand! (139:1–18).

And if you dare, pray as David did, "Search me, O God, and know my heart; test me and know my anxious thoughts. Point out anything in me that offends you, and lead me along the path of everlasting life" (Ps 139:23–24).

ABOUT THE AUTHOR

Brian Ming started writing songs and poems at age sixteen. His love for writing music led to authoring fiction, often coupling songs with storytelling. His first novel and public debut, *Snow Sometimes Falls,* received great reviews and quickly became an Amazon Bestseller. He is also the author of several short stories and the *Future Kingdom Series* as well as the *Secret Heart Series.*

Brian is a sought-after speaker and worship leader whose passion to teach others how to develop their God-given creativity to the fullest has inspired millions. He currently resides with his wife, Kristen, and two of their three children in Colorado Springs, CO.

You can learn more about Brian's ministry by visiting: https://unveiledworship.co/.

ALSO BY BRIAN MING

Secret Heart of God (Secret Heart Series, Book 1)

Secret Heart of a King (Secret Heart Series, Book 3)

Snow Sometimes Falls

Everlove (The Future Kingdom Series, Book 1)

Liongate (The Future Kingdom Series, Book 2)

Everlove (The Future Kingdom Series, Book 3)